NO
Ordinary
VIEW

NO *Ordinary* VIEW

A SEASON OF FAITH & MISSION IN THE HIMALAYAS

NAOMI REED

Authentic

For Darren, Stephen, Chris and Jeremy who not only lived the story with me, they also gave me the space I needed to write it down. And for all those who wanted to know what really happened in the final chapter of our seventh monsoon. Special thanks to Penny Reeve, who had the courage to tell me the things I needed to hear. And also to Tony Woodruff who used his fine-tooth comb so thoroughly on this manuscript.

'So we fix our eyes not on what is seen, but on what is unseen. For what is seen is temporary, but what is unseen is eternal.'
(2 Corinthians 4:18)

Contents

PROLOGUE

HIDDEN TREASURES

It was a clear afternoon in June and we pulled in to a town called Rubyvale, 325 kilometres west of Rockhampton. The ground was hard and all three boys complained as they hammered away at the tent pegs. In between the hammering I heard them call out to me, wanting to know why we had stopped in Rubyvale. I smiled to myself. After the lures of the Queensland coastline, it was a reasonable question. I pulled the bags out of the boot and walked back over to where they stood by the tent.

'Have a look over there,' I said, pointing to huge mounds of discarded dirt beyond the wire fence of the camping ground. 'Rubyvale is an old mining town and it's well known for its sapphires. And see that sign – it's pointing to a working mine and some old miners' cottages.' I watched their heads turn, but their expressions didn't change. So I increased my own cheerfulness. 'We can go there tomorrow and look for sapphires.'

Whether it was the appeal of the sapphires or Darren's timely arrival with the sausages, the subject changed and soon they were throwing the football to each other near the barbecue area, laughing at the way it bounced off the dry ground.

Then the following day we joined the fossickers. We met up with a tour group and were taken all the way down an old disused mine. The stairs were rickety and the tunnels were long and damp. Jeremy kept stopping to look behind him and I kept bumping into him in the patches of dim light. At one point our tour guide stopped and began to explain to us the appeal and the value of gemstones. Then she turned off her torch and asked us to look in the direction that she'd been pointing. At first, it was merely darkness, the darkness of a tunnel twenty metres below the earth, a place where the sunshine had never entered. Then, slowly, as our eyes focused, we began to see a line of sapphires, as blue and as brilliant as the sky way above us. Within the darkness of the tunnel they shone. They stood out amidst the mud of their surroundings. Their facets gleamed, almost incongruous in an otherwise earthen wall. It was, strangely, a completely unexpected sight. At the Whitsundays, on a tour of the Great Barrier Reef, we had expected beauty and we had found it. But in Rubyvale, we had not particularly expected beauty and yet found it, in the darkness.

Later that morning, we bought a bucket of earth that had been extracted from a working mine and we took it to a table and a nearby water trough in order to search through it for the same kind of gleam. Slowly, we poured it onto a large tray and then rinsed away the smaller particles of dust and dirt. Then we up-ended the pile onto a table and began to sift through it with tweezers, peering at each piece of stone carefully, just in case we had missed a gleam. It was painstaking, delicate work. It was mind-numbing. Soon, Jeremy abandoned the search and went off chasing a lizard. Chris and Stephen persisted but they were also drawn to the office where they had caught a glimpse of Coke bottles in the fridge. Darren and I kept going but our eyes grew tired and our backs ached. The sun rose higher in the sky and our T-shirts began to stick to our backs. After a while, we couldn't remember which bits we had sifted through and which bits we hadn't.

As I leaned over the wooden trestle, staring at the dirt and thinking about the treasures that might be hiding there, fragments of a long-forgotten conversation came back to me. Two years earlier, I had been walking with Gillian across the ridges near our home town of Dhulikhel, Nepal. It had been pouring with rain and the sound of it splattering on our parkas and pelting through the nearby corn crops almost drowned out her words.

'The thing is,' Gillian called across to me, 'when the sun is out and the day is bright, everyone wants to walk. When the sun is out, walking is easy.' I peered through the stream of water that was running down my fringe and made vain attempts to redirect it from my chin.

Gillian wiped the water from her face and continued, 'Walking in the sunshine might be easy, it might be nice, but you don't find the treasures.'

She told me of a time when she had been walking through mountains in Canada in pouring rain. She described the noise of the rain and the feel of being alone with the elements. Then, she told me about turning around and seeing a cougar right in front of her.

'It stood there, stock still and I knew that it was the most beautiful thing that I had ever seen; him and me in the pouring rain,' Gillian turned and smiled at me again. 'You don't find cougars in the sunshine. You find them in the darkness.'

That morning in Dhulikhel, Nepal, I had returned home, rediscovered dryness and read from Isaiah 45:2–3:

> I will go before you and will level the mountains; I will break down gates of bronze and cut through bars of iron. I will give you the treasures of darkness, riches stored in secret places, so that you may know that I am the LORD, the God of Israel, who summons you by name.

I had sat there on the back porch of my home, stared at the clouds and wondered about treasures. I wondered whether

God had treasures for me to find within the pain and darkness that surrounded us in those years in Nepal. Ten years of civil war, a deteriorating health system, an economic crisis and a political stalemate. It was a background of hopelessness for the lives of our Nepali friends and the community that we lived in. In such a setting, how could God reveal his nature? And in such a setting, how could God call me by name? I didn't know. I didn't think it was possible.

1

PLANT DOWN

On a bitterly cold January day in 2004 we climbed into INF's old green van, wedged ourselves between the cane bookshelves and the new gas cooker, and made the journey to our new house in Dhulikhel. The journey from Kathmandu to Dhulikhel is only 30 kilometres but on that day it took nearly two hours.

The van pottered along behind a steady stream of overcrowded taxis and trucks on their way to Tibet. Motorbikes darted in and out, impatient to be out of the valley. Horns bleated out, demanding immediate attention and cows raised bored eyelashes and then moved slowly out of the way. Inside the van, our three boys raised the pitch of their voices.

'Mum! Can I have my own room?'

'Stephen! Get off my foot, you're standing on it.'

'That's not my foot, that's the bike tyre.'

We all nudged ourselves two centimetres to the left to make more room for the bike tyre. Outside, the succession of concrete buildings and bazaar areas were slowly giving way to paddy fields and rivers. The road wound to the right and began the ascent out of the Kathmandu valley. Heavily terraced hills now laid their arms around the road. As our eyes followed the curves we saw mud houses sitting in rows along the ridges, catching the sunlight and giving us a tiny glimpse of the people who lived and toiled there.

'I still can't see Dhulikhel,' said Chris as he pushed himself closer to the window. 'And why are we stopping?' He squirmed into the place between Stephen's arm and the bike tyre and stared out at the crowds of people outside the window. 'And what are all those army men doing?'

'It's just another checkpoint,' I said. 'They're making sure that everything's OK.' Then I manoeuvred myself so that I could rest my hand on his shoulder. He looked up and I smiled back. 'Not much further now. We have to get through Banepa and then we should be able to see Dhulikhel over the next ridge.'

The three boys each strained further forward, determined to be the first. Even 2-year-olds will detect the essence of a competition, long before they can put the answer into words. Stephen, at 8, had the best chance.

'I see it!' He pointed wildly at the township on the far hill and was rewarded with complaints from the other two. They evened out the point score by being the first to see the bus stop and the hospital, the buffalo at the corner and the banana man pushing his trolley up the lane. Then, not to be put off, Stephen saw the road that led to his new school and the king's statue. Chris saw the football field and Jeremy saw a duck, so Stephen saw the prison and the army camp.

It would have gone on like that, except that everybody saw the little turn-off that led up the hill to our new house. Everybody scrambled out, a tangle of legs and bikes and cane bookshelves, and everybody raced to the front door, as fast as their legs had ever raced, as excited as they'd ever been. Our new chapter in Dhulikhel was about to begin.

The padlock turned easily and we tumbled in, three boys and two parents, eager for the new page, longing to know what would unfold there and impatient for it to begin. We'd spent too many years talking about it and no time living it. That would all change in a moment.

The first thing I noticed was that the plumbing wasn't working. Both bathrooms were swimming in an inch of murky brown water and both sinks and toilets were blocked by clumps of plaster. The smell of dead fish wafted out into the hall. Walking into the kitchen added to the nasal assault. The house had been left empty for three months, which meant that the mould had worked its way through the cupboards. As I opened each of the cupboards in turn, the white growth seemed to have replaced the wood. Indeed, the wood beneath the sink fell away as I touched it, as rotten as the remains of a white ant attack. In each of the bedrooms, painter's debris lined the threadbare carpet and dust had settled onto the few pieces of furniture that had been left behind by the landlord. We investigated every room and searched vainly for a power point or a light switch that worked. Instead, we found electric shocks in the bathroom.

'Don't touch it!' I yelled, a split second too late.

Stephen and I both stared down at his finger as if the buzzing should have been visible. I gave it a rub while he made his decision. 'That's it,' he said, 'I'm never going in *there* again.'

The boys claimed the three beds in the largest bedroom upstairs and began unearthing forgotten toys and books out of the blue barrels. They hadn't seen the contents since we had packed the barrels four months earlier, just prior to leaving Australia, so they were understandably elated. I tried not to think about the dust settling on the precious contents and went in search of clean-up materials.

Three hours later, the kitchen was clean and the beds were made. But with each passing hour, the chill that had begun on our ascent out of the valley, seemed to be descending in degrees. The adaptor on our portable heater refused to work in any of the power points. The gas on our two-ringed burner needed another connection in order to function. So we sat

there in the kitchen and ate cold sausages out of a tin for dinner – with our hats and gloves on. We looked around us at the
bare walls, the worn brown tiles and then at each other. Even
Darren admitted that it was a bit grim.

I thought that it was more than grim. As I looked at the bare
walls that enclosed us, my head began to feel as bare as the
room that we sat in. Even worse than the bareness inside was
the bareness outside, because outside of the empty walls, we
knew nobody. We kept our hats and gloves on as we crawled
into bed, hoping that the sunrise would bring with it some
beauty.

It did. The previous day had been cold and bleak, a winter's
day in Dhulikhel where the fog and cloud had sat so low that
they buried the Himalayas. The horizon that we saw out of the
back windows was merely the shape of the banana trees in the
back garden. Beyond the banana trees sat another dark shape
of a building in the next garden. A cow mooed from beneath
its cover. That was all.

We woke the next morning and called the kids into our bed.
They crawled in under the heavy blue quilt and tucked themselves into the cosiest corners. They waited till they had
stopped shivering and then started to wonder what the bird
was that they could hear singing outside our window. That
was when we remembered the Himalayas.

Chris leapt out to draw the curtains and then dived back in
before anyone else could claim his warm spot. We all leaned
forward and rubbed our eyes as if we needed to refocus the
image. Across the entire horizon framed by our window lay a
panorama of white mountains. The rays of the sun were in the
process of lighting up each peak one by one, until they glowed
as if in the beam of a gigantic spotlight. We lay there, momentarily silent, as we searched for words that could describe the
sight. Then we began to hazard guesses as to which peak
would glow next. The peaks took their turn until, fifteen

minutes later, the show was over and the lights were all on. The day could begin.

For the boys, that didn't mean breakfast. That meant racing outside to explore their new back garden. The chill in the air blew in through the back door and the frost was so thick on the ground that their shoes left crunch marks all over the garden. It was freezing, but to them it was full of possibilities. From the back porch the land sloped away into four large over-grown terraces, not quite ready for planting crops. In between the terraces were a dozen established trees – plums and oranges, grapefruits and bananas. In between the trees were the kind of magical places where boys immediately see hide-outs and dens, forts and castles. They got to work straight away.

I followed them later with my bucket of washing. I scram-bled down past the first two terraces, thankful for a well-placed orange tree that slowed my descent. I rested at the plum tree, replaced some washing that had fallen out and looked around me. Below the terraces was a large swamp in which the boys were now retrieving old grapefruits and pine cones to stockpile in their forts. Cries of delight echoed around the garden with each new glorious find. I spied the washing line, cleverly placed in the only patch of sun in the garden and set to work to empty my bucket.

Other people enjoy scrubbing bathrooms until they are sparkling white or making beds with perfectly folded corners. Not me. If I ever had to choose a household task, it would always be hanging out washing. Out there in the sunshine, I can catch the breeze, spy an early butterfly and dream about tomorrow while still feeling vaguely useful. I could also, in Dhulikhel, keep my eye on the swamp and check that Jeremy hadn't fallen in head first.

On that very first morning in Dhulikhel, I hung it out slowly and carefully. I lined up all the socks in perfect order and gave myself plenty of time to dream. There were no disasters in the swamp, so that was OK as well. As I hung, I took in my surroundings. The house we had moved into was the middle one in a set of three identical Nepali townhouses. Through the strings of clothesline I could see their white-washed walls and the dark red trim on the windows. The garden to the left of ours was immaculately kept. Neat hedges bordered Himalayan grasses and an assortment of lilies. A red sari was already blowing in the breeze, telling me that they were early risers. We had met the various occupants of that house the day before during the electric shock episode: the Nepali Vice Chancellor of Kathmandu University and his friendly wife, Urmila, and their assortment of relatives.

To my right, the garden was well planted out with winter vegetables. Three neat rows of vegetables led up to the house which was framed by roses and climbing ivy. On the back porch I could just make out some cane chairs and the backs of our Australian neighbours. John and Margaret, an older couple, taught engineering at the university and English at a local school. We had also met them during our search for clean-up materials. They, happily, were in possession of the only vacuum cleaner in Dhulikhel. We availed ourselves of it.

The three back gardens merged into one large and enchanting area bordered only by hedges and orange trees. I looked around me and knew that the boys were going to love it. They were already talking about the mudslide they could make when the monsoon hit Dhulikhel that year. But as well as the mud, there were mountains. From every viewpoint, the Langtang Range of the Himalayas was beckoning me from the other side of the valley. It was calling me to raise my eyes and notice the distant as well as the proximate. I could do that. I knew that I could.

I picked up my bucket and slowly made my way back up to the house. In some ways, I was feeling positive about the adjustments that I knew were ahead of us. We had already lived in Nepal for three years in the nineties. During that particular chapter we had lived in Pokhara, a town 200 kilometres to the west of Kathmandu, and Darren and I had worked as physiotherapists in the local government and leprosy hospitals. The highlight of those years was the arrival of Stephen, our tiny blonde son, whose presence seemed to make life both infinitely harder and yet infinitely more delightful in a country where only 30 per cent of the population have access to clean drinking water and medical services.

I thought of those years as I made my way back up past the terraces. Being back in the Himalayas somehow made them more vivid. It was almost as if those years became more tangible and real to me than the intervening ones that we had lived in the Blue Mountains, west of Sydney. Then, I remembered the water shortages and the power cuts and the frustration of operating in another language. I remembered the terrible ache in my belly every time I went to buy bananas. I remembered the fog of trying to develop deep and lasting relationships.

In some ways, the memories gave me courage. If I could do it then, I could do it now. And besides, this time I already had a reasonable grasp of the language. I already knew that a dozen nice bananas should cost 25 rupees (about 22 pence) and I could easily and politely ask for what I wanted. I could even discuss weather patterns, job satisfaction or family dynamics while I waited for the change. Or maybe I just thought I could . . . Either way, I was in a better place. I wasn't brand new like I'd been in the nineties; I wasn't brand new to the country or the culture or the language. But as soon as the reassuring thoughts came, the daunting thoughts came as well. I wasn't brand new to the country or the culture or the language but I was brand new to Dhulikhel and I didn't know anyone at all. I was starting all over again, in a culture and language that wasn't my own. I wished, momentarily, that I could spend the next three years hanging out my washing.

Three days after we moved in, Darren began work as a physiotherapy tutor at Dhulikhel Medical Institute (DMI), the recently opened and only physio training school in the country. The job was not only perfect for him, but it was also a role that he'd been preparing for in various ways for the last ten years. He piled as many textbooks as he could into his rucksack and then eased himself and his bicycle out of our front door. On the same day, Stephen began Year 3 at Kathmandu University Prep School (KUPS), a Nepali school located on the next mountain. He fiddled with the belt on his new uniform and pulled his hat down further before hugging me and following Darren out of the door.

Chris, Jeremy and I waved to them both from the gate and watched till they turned the corner at the bottom of our hill, Darren on his mountain bike and Stephen on the local bus. I could just make out Stephen's blonde head amongst the sea of dark ones, as the bus rattled past the army camp and disappeared into the bazaar. I kept staring for a while and then turned my gaze back to the place where we stood – at the verge of the gate, nearly out but not quite.

We looked at each other and I thought about our options. We could go back into the house and start preschool but I hadn't unpacked the preschool bag. We could stay in the courtyard and ride bikes but the bike tyres were flat. We could go into the back garden and dig a flower bed but I didn't have a spade. That meant that we had to go out. We had to begin to make relationships. Although daunting, it was time to begin.

Dhulikhel bazaar winds the whole way through the town. From the main market, it carries along on top of the ridge, past the schools, the prison, the football field and the post office. That morning, the road seemed to be mostly dirt and mostly filled with pedestrians. Once or twice, we saw a vehicle, but it seemed to be the exception rather than the norm. Groups of Nepalis were walking to the temple carrying their *puja* offerings and others were walking to the bazaar carrying their buffalo milk to sell. Hordes of school children streamed past, each carrying a wooden clipboard and one pencil. Then after the children, came the women, slower and quieter, carrying their first *doko* (cane basket) full of grass cuttings to feed their buffalo. Young boys on bicycles announced their presence with bells and then tried to dodge the pedestrians or the even less predictable livestock.

Jeremy and Chris didn't try to dodge the livestock – they tried to catch them. Dozens of goats were lining the road on leads, having been brought in to find fresh patches of grass. They were easy to pat. Much more enticing than them though, were the baby goats that gambolled unfettered between them. Patting a leaping goat kid not only gave the boys more points, but also gave them more energy to carry on around the next corner. And who knew what delights would be around the next corner – tiny ducklings and noisy roosters and snorting pigs and enormous buffalo.

I watched the boys as they darted across the road in front of me. They stopped and started, finding sticks and precious stones, taking their time to dig another hole in the road before the next goat sighting. From behind me, the sun rose higher and reflected off their blonde heads until they looked like fireflies bent on a path of their own design, distracted by the moment and moved by delight rather than intent on a purpose.

I learnt from them and slowed down my pace. I took in my surroundings and thought about the very beginnings of relationships. I motioned a *namaste* (greeting) to the lady in the tiny vegetable shop. She put her hands together and smiled back. Her daughter bent double to get out of the carved wooden opening at the front of the shop and then walked with us for a while, showing me the school and the *mo-mo* shop. Beyond the *mo-mo* shop was another small shop selling fabric. The boys were still engaged, so I slipped off my *chappals* (sandals) and stepped quietly inside. Inside the shop were rows of brightly coloured cloth, reds and greens and swirling patterns, the perfect trigger to get me dreaming of curtains. I was engrossed by the colours and I scanned the room, trying to take in each one, determined not to miss a possibility. Then, just as I was reaching towards a fabric in rich burgundy, the sounds of sleep invaded my consciousness. Quiet sounds, yet sleepy sounds; breathing that knows not how it sounds, nor even cares. I looked over at the other side of the shop and saw the *sahuji* (shopkeeper). He lay curled up on a thin mattress, his hair over his face and given over to dreams – blissful, undisturbed dreams.

Jeremy and Chris came bouncing into the shop, talking about ducklings and I waved at them to be quiet. They hesitated, saw the stillness of the *sahuji* and were instantly silent. They sat down on the little stools and stared. They had never entered a stranger's sleep before. I also stared and as I did, I began to sense something new, something very relaxing – something that spoke of the pace of life. Don't hurry, take it easy, watch the goats, find precious stones, follow the sunshine, talk to the passers-by, make friends . . . and sleep if you need to.

I stepped back outside and watched an old lady pass by. She was wrinkled and tired, carrying her pile of firewood on her back. Her bright red blouse and patterned sari were almost hidden by the load. Her body was bent double with the effort and her bare, calloused feet gave the clues to her days. Our eyes met and we smiled. It was something. It was the beginning. I wasn't yet making relationships but I was doing something. I was planting myself in the new soil. I was letting my well-shod feet sink into it.

Much later, as I sat in our new cane chair on the back porch of our house, I read from Jeremiah 29:4–7:

> This is what the LORD Almighty, the God of Israel, says to all those I carried into exile from Jerusalem to Babylon: 'Build houses and settle down; plant gardens and eat what they produce. Marry and have sons and daughters; find wives for your sons and give your daughters in marriage, so that they too may have sons and daughters. Increase in number there; do not decrease. Also, seek the peace and prosperity of the city to which I have carried you into exile. Pray to the LORD for it, because if it prospers, you too will prosper.'

As I read, I learnt that prior to this passage, the Israelites had found themselves in Babylon and the prophet Jeremiah had written to tell them that they would be in exile there for seventy years. He told them that therefore they needed to settle down and get on with life, rather than continuing to long for Zion. On that winter's afternoon, after our first foray into the bazaar, it seemed like a helpful passage to read. Once again, I was in a new and strange land, a land that at first seemed beyond my grasp. And I needed to plant myself deeply there, trusting that that was where God had put me – for a time and for a purpose. In the planting, I had to somehow stop longing for my other land – for our home back in the Blue Mountains, with the glorious back deck and the sounds of friendly cricket matches and the buzz of conversations and the smell of barbecues from down the street. Somehow, I had to gradually ease those pictures from my mind and replace them with the new ones, the ones on the Dhulikhel ridge, the ones yet to unfold. And in the planting, I had to pray. I had to pray for Nepal like the Israelites had to pray for Babylon.

There were similarities but there were also differences. Unlike the Israelites, we had not been sent to Nepal in order to remain there in exile for seventy years. On the contrary, our purposes and our motivations as well as our time scale were quite different. We had returned to Nepal for a specific three-year term in order to teach physiotherapy at the Dhulikhel Medical Institute (DMI). We had been sent there by Interserve, a Christian seconding agency, who then teamed us up to work with the International Nepal Fellowship (INF). The INF was well-known to us because of our years of service with them in Nepal during the nineties. As a mission, its commitment to poverty alleviation and service of the people, through medical work and training, was second to none. For all these reasons, we were highly motivated on our return to Nepal. Not only did we want to be there but we also wanted to become deeply planted in our new community. In all of our living and breathing and service, we wanted to be able to share the love of Jesus with those whom we met. We believed strongly that God had sent us there for that very purpose.

We believed it and we wanted it more than anything but the depth of my humanity faltered at the extent of the work involved. Over the next few weeks, as I began the tenuous links that might possibly lead to relationship, I often saw the road up ahead and wanted to flee. I stared at the lady with the heavy earrings and wondered whether she was the same one that I had met the day before by the tap. I watched the group of lads walk by and I wondered whether any of them had been in church the previous Saturday. I sat in the little vegetable shop and couldn't remember how many daughters the shop-keeper had, if any.

One day, as I walked with the boys past the pipal tree at the bottom of our hill, I watched a group of Nepali women walking past, their scarves blowing in the wind and the sounds of their conversation blending with the colours of their scarves. I watched the way their bodies moved in step with each other and I felt the sounds of their laughter, their connection. I watched something that I myself didn't have and I felt the weight of the emptiness around me.

It sat heavily and, once again, I longed for Zion, for a place where I belonged and felt comfortable. But within the longing, the words of Jeremiah kept coming back to me, over and over again, 'Seek the peace and prosperity of the city to which I have carried you . . . Pray to the Lord for it.' Over the next few weeks and months, I prayed and I prayed and it did seem that somehow, in the process of praying for Dhulikhel, my heart moved in.

2

THREE TOMATOES AND
AN ONION

While I was busy praying and planting, I was also sorting through the details of life in a foreign country. The most pressing detail, for me, was finding food for all of us. We had brought a box of supplies with us from Kathmandu on the initial journey, but it only took about a week of breakfasts for us to come to the bottom of our tin of powdered milk. As I stared at the shiny aluminium poking through the powder at the base of the tin, I knew that I had to find someone with a buffalo – and quite quickly. In Nepal, buffalo are the main source of thick creamy milk, so I had to become a destination point for one of the men who walked the path each morning at 6 a.m. swinging their milk cans. It all sounds very simple, but it wasn't. It's not like searching for something in a Western country. There's no newspaper advertisement or flyer in the mailbox, telling you about the latest buffalo milk for 65p a litre. There wasn't even any mailbox – let alone the Internet or the Yellow Pages. Not only did we not have a mailbox, we didn't even have an address. At first glance in Nepal, it often feels like there is no system.

But that's because the first glance is always from a Western framework. There is always a system in Nepal and the system is always relational. You don't need advertisements and flyers and the Internet when you have friends and relations. If you don't have friends and relations, then you find them as soon as possible. It's the only way to survive – because they are the source of all things good. Our delightful Nepali neighbour, Urmila, soon became that source.

She introduced us to the man who brought her milk every morning. He was small and chirpy and, in true Brahmin style, always wore his *topi* (Nepali hat) perched carefully over his lined forehead. At first, he would arrive at our doorstep, place the milk can carefully on the tiles and then ring the bell as loudly and as frequently as he could. It was 5.30 a.m. and he had been up for hours milking the animals and then walking into town from his mud home in the next village. It always seemed to vaguely surprise him that Darren had, quite clearly, not been up for hours. Darren had, in fact, emerged from sleep at the precise moment that the bell rang. So, unfortunately, had the boys, tumbling out of sleep and down the stairs in one fluid motion, always wanting to be the first to greet the visitor.

It didn't take us long to work out a system where we placed the saucepan out on the tiles the night before and then discovered fresh buffalo milk in the morning, just in time for breakfast. The pot would go on the gas cooker and pasteurise before our eyes, the smells of wood fire from the milkman's hut merging with the milk vapour until we were all reaching for mugs of Horlicks. After the Horlicks urge had been satisfied, we then poured oats into the remainder of the milk pot and filled our insides, daily, with steaming porridge.

The milkman proved to be more than a useful contact. As well as his buffalo, he also had a small grove of orange trees on his Himalayan terrace, a thriving market garden and the only flour mill in Dhulikhel, all with a view of Everest. Once a week he would arrive at our house with 10 kilograms of flour, 5 kilograms of potatoes and 2 kilograms of oranges – as well as the milk can. I was delighted. I could almost feel my shoulders sigh with relief, knowing that they wouldn't have to carry that load up the hill from the bazaar.

All the rest of the food possibilities were to be found down the hill, in the Dhulikhel bazaar. The first and most exciting possibility we found was the doughnut man. He sat in a tiny shop on the street and made rounds of flour, lining them up in rows before dropping them into a huge vat of oil on a kerosene burner on the street. He then reached into the oil with a long stick and retrieved them all, like a dozen quoits on a javelin. Straight from the stick, they were dripping and delicious. An hour later, after they'd been wrapped in newspaper and carried back up our hill and into our kitchen, they were not quite so delicious. We'd forgotten the way that cold oil forms globules on the insides of your mouth.

Further up from the doughnut man was our local *sahuji*, sitting happily in his shop and surrounded by shelves of food in a space the size of a small bedroom. We would approach his shop with anticipation, always wondering whether we would find something new amidst the layers of soap and toothpaste and spices and peanuts. Our anticipation would then settle slowly, as we also did on the cane stools in front of the counter. As we leant forward on our stools, our eyes would begin the slow process of scanning the shelves for something tasty and edible. While we scanned, invariably a crowd would gather around us to observe our purchases. They would stand or sit nearby, quietly watching or sometimes commenting to each other if our purchases were unfathomable.

The first time I asked the *sahuji* for toilet paper a crowd of women pressed in around me. After some careful, albeit quiet, explaining on my part the *sahuji* nodded at me to show that he had understood what I needed. Then he reached down for his long stick and waved it high in the air until it touched the highest point in the shop, way above the other shelves. From this advantageous position, he gave a clever flick and the mysterious package toppled off the highest shelf and landed neatly below in the sack of yellow lentils. The long years of being uncalled for had added to its strange appearance. He dusted it down and handed it over. The women crowded around. They poked at it and prodded it. 'But what's it for?' they asked. That day, I tried to think up reasons to delay my answer. I was already strange enough.

After the doughnut man and the *sahuji*, and before the doughnuts cooled, we would stop in at the tiny vegetable shop. Bagmati, whose name I eventually remembered, always sat in the centre, immediately behind the weighing scales that hung from the ceiling. From her position she could reach every item in the shop and weigh it on the scales, at the same time as peering out through the carved wooden opening to greet the passers-by. From daybreak to nightfall, through summer and winter, there she was, sitting and smiling. There was one other stool in the shop and it perched between the wooden crates of cauliflowers and cucumbers. I would step over the crate of tomatoes, dodge the bananas that hung from the ceiling and settle myself down for a chat while she weighed out a week's worth of fruit and vegetables for us.

One day, while we were discussing Bagmati's mysterious stomach ailment and searching for a less mouldy cauliflower, an older lady peered in at the door, asking for tomatoes. She looped her worn red sari back into position and said that she needed a quarter of a kilo.

'*Panch rupiya*,' said Bagmati, in the voice of one who has bargained over the price of tomatoes for a thousand hours. Bagmati knew, and I knew, that 5 rupees (4 pence) for 3 tomatoes was the going rate. The Nepali woman also knew. She knew, but she tried anyway. '*Teen rupiya*,' she said – 3 rupees would be better.

Bagmati shook her head and the woman repeated the exchange. The exchange, repeated, ended at the same point that it had 7 minutes earlier – 5 rupees or nothing. The woman finally decided, after one more try, to buy 2 tomatoes instead. She handed over 3 rupees and then carefully folded the 2 tomatoes into the waist fold of her sari and bent forward to exit the shop. She slowly picked up her *doko* of grass cuttings and made her way back up the hill.

I watched the sway of her load and I listened to the sound of her *chappals* flip-flopping on the muddy path. The sound echoed within the shop as I returned to my ½ kilogram of eggplant, ¼ kilogram of beans and 2 kilograms of apples. I had already purchased half a pumpkin and a full kilogram of tomatoes, not to mention the cauliflowers. I looked down at the bulges in my rucksack and it seemed, momentarily, obscene.

What sort of world is this where 2 rupees is the difference between a meal and the absence of a meal? What could she possibly cook for her family with 2 tomatoes? Perhaps she already has onions, I thought to myself. Then I proceeded to buy 2 kilograms of them myself. My bill came to 324 rupees (£2.79). I carefully counted out the change and then tried to lift my load. The bulges were so excessive that I could hardly get it onto my back. I squatted down to ease it on and then bid farewell to Bagmati, moving slowly, somehow wanting to avoid the other woman up ahead. I would have moved slowly anyway. That many kilograms of fruit and vegetables weighed me down ordinarily, let alone with the additional burden of guilt – which weighed heavier than all of them.

Living in the midst of destitute poverty began, once again, to gnaw away at my insides until it felt like there was not a single question that had a single answer. The questions and the answers merged into a sigh that had morning and noon and night within it. The sighs then crept up within me and overwhelmed me at every step of the journey. They were hiding in the vegetable shop and they were with me in the bazaar and they were even waiting at our front door.

One day, we were walking to the hospital to meet Darren after work. A lady with a baby approached me and we chatted for about ten minutes as we walked along and through the bazaar. The smells of incense wafted out from the shops and various *sahujis* touted their wares. We smiled at them and continued our conversation. It would have been more unusual if we hadn't chatted. We talked about our children and we talked about the weather. Then she asked me if I would take her baby.

I looked down at the baby, who lay strapped to the woman's back in an old green *kasto* (shawl). Her brown eyes stared out at me from beneath her red woollen hat and her chin was covered in dribble. She smelled like a pile of musty blankets.

The baby was 6 months old and the woman's third daughter. Her husband had deserted her after the third girl was born because as a Hindu he needed a son to perform his funeral rights. The woman now earned 30 rupees (26 pence) a day working in the rice fields. It wasn't enough for four of them. Her eldest daughter, at the age of 9, was working each day washing dishes in the bazaar. She earned her keep. Her second daughter, at 4 years old, was staying at home each day to mind the baby. None of the girls would ever go to school. I looked back down at the baby, as I considered the woman's words. '*Dinos, malai.*' Help me.

Help me. I slowly reached for the baby and I tucked her into the curve in my elbow. She fitted perfectly. I looked down at her face and I watched her breathing. I felt it on my skin. Then I smiled at her and her little cheek dimpled as she smiled back. It made me smile more and I held her a little bit closer. Then I passed her back – and I told the woman that she had a beautiful baby. I asked her where she lived and the next time I was passing through, I gave her a bagful of clothes. It wasn't what she wanted. But it was all that I thought I could do.

On another day we had a knock at our front door and I opened it to find a young woman standing on the doorstep with a baby in her arms. She was barefoot and it was the middle of winter. I felt the chill in the breeze as I greeted her. She told me that a fire had destroyed her home and that her husband was in hospital with severe burns. She said that her little boy had died in the fire and then, she just looked at me and said, *'Dinos, malai.'* Help me.

Help me. Help me to know what to do. I gave her warm clothing and a cup of tea and something for the baby. I told her that my husband was at the hospital; perhaps he could help her husband. Then, after more deliberations, I said goodbye and closed the door behind her – to keep the warmth inside.

At other times I could do more and still other times I could do less. Srijana used to come to our house twice a week in order to cut the grass from the terraces in our back garden. She would creep in noiselessly from over the hill behind the swamp, her empty *doko* swinging from the braided rope around her forehead. I would be emptying the scraps into the pit below the orange tree and catch a glimpse of her red sari as she swept her sickle in arches across the overgrown grass. It took two hours of squatting to cut enough grass to fill a *doko* and it took three *dokos* of grass to satisfy a hungry buffalo. It happened every single day.

Sometimes she would break for a drink and I would join her on our back porch. As we gazed at our Himalayan view, I heard about her family. I learnt that her husband had no work and that they and their children lived in a single room in the mud hut with his parents. The parents also had no income apart from the money that they made from selling the buffalo milk. Srijana spent her days gathering grass for the buffalo and firewood for the open fire that they cooked on. She was often hungry. She didn't say, *'Dinos, malai.'*

She didn't ask for help – yet I gave it to her anyway. I offered her work in our house. I offered it tentatively, not sure if she wanted it. If she could wash the dishes and keep the floors clean I could pay her enough money to buy rice for the family and send her children to school. She smiled, and as she did it was as if the sun shone out of her eyes. I think she wanted it.

She wanted it, but she was terribly nervous. On the first morning, after an enthusiastic greeting, she laboured over the dishes. She seemed to take all morning to wash five of them. I asked her later if everything was alright.

'Oh yes,' she replied in Nepali, still shining. 'But this was the first time in my life that I have ever held anything breakable.' She paused as she admitted it. 'I was very frightened of dropping them – so I held on as tightly as I could. Do you think it will get quicker?'

She did indeed get quicker and she quickly became indispensable. She became another one of our 'friends and relations'. On lazy afternoons when the jobs were all done, we would all escape via the swamp and head over the hill to her mud house. Their front step would capture the late afternoon sun and we would sit there drinking *chiya* (Nepali tea) while the children all played in the paddy fields.

It sounds blissful and very often that's exactly how life in Dhulikhel was. The pace was slow, the conversations were important and the hot *chiya* was always on tap and always relaxing. But at other times the blissfulness was eroded by the questions that plagued me. Am I doing as much as I can do in this situation? Who else could I or should I be helping? How is the man with polio going to survive this winter? Which ones are the genuine requests, or are they all genuine? Which ones are the neediest requests, or are they all needy? If we help the young man at church, will the rest of the congregation continue to come to church merely for what they can get out of the *bideshis* (foreigners)? And . . . if I were them, would I not also?

In the March of 2004, Philip Yancey came to speak at our INF Conference in Pokhara. It was a memorable week. The Maoists called yet more transport *bandhs* (strikes) and so we walked for two hours to get to the conference one morning. One afternoon we rounded up all our children and sent them home in the ambulance to avoid the oncoming *bandh*. As well as that, the clouds moved in and covered the Himalayas for the entire week. Philip began to question their existence but fortunately he remained open to the questions that we had for him.

I remember Maurice's question. Maurice is a good friend of ours and at that stage he was working as an anaesthetist in a smaller mission hospital in the hills of Nepal. Prior to coming to Nepal he had worked hard as a consultant anaesthetist in New Zealand. He had devoted his life to saving the lives of others and to keeping patients alive. The surgeon may cut them open and fix the parts that aren't functioning, the nurse may keep it clean and prevent infection, but the anaesthetist keeps the patient alive. It's his job, more than anyone else's. Maurice knew how to do it and he knew why he did it. The reason he woke up every morning was to keep people alive and that's what he did.

But in Nepal, it all changed. In Nepal, Maurice saw people die who wouldn't have died in the West. In Nepal, Maurice cried. One day, quite near his house, a Nepali child was playing beside an open water tank and was caught inside. A colleague found the child, realised she was not breathing, and scrambled down the hill, carrying her in his arms. At that moment, Maurice happened to be passing by and he raced alongside them. They arrived quickly at the hospital which was just next door. Maurice then did everything that he could do with the resources that he had – and given his expertise that was extensive – but the child died in his arms. He couldn't do what he'd been trained to do.

The questions plagued him in the early hours of the mornings. He wondered if he could have saved her if he'd been in the West and had access to Western technology. He wondered if he could have saved her if he'd walked by moments earlier. He wondered if he could have saved her, period. Weeks later, the nights were still long and the questions still haunted him. So he asked Philip for some godly wisdom.

Philip acknowledged the question with a nod of his head and a sigh. 'You know, you can't save the world – you can only do the best you can with what's in front of you.' He smiled at Maurice, 'And as you go, point to the one who can save the world.'

I took the answer with me and mulled it over as we sat on the long bus ride back to Dhulikhel. As I stared down at the Trisuli River thirty metres below us the words began to rebuild the wall that my questions had eroded. Philip was right, I couldn't save the world; I could only do the best I could with those in front of me. In Dhulikhel I couldn't meet all the needs of those who said to me, '*Dinos, Malai,*' but perhaps I could, very quietly, point to the one who could save the world. I closed my eyes and repeated the words to myself as the sway of the bus took us back home to Dhulikhel.

3

LIFT YOUR EYES

By April, we were feeling much more settled in Dhulikhel. We had found enough pieces of cane furniture to fill up the empty spaces of our home. The boys had made a cubby hole beneath the stairs and I had made curtains out of the burgundy fabric. We'd sorted out our food supply and begun to recognise and chat to our neighbours. We'd even settled into a local Nepali church that met on a Saturday morning near the bus park. As well as that, Darren had settled into his tutoring job at the university and was coming home with stories of his keen young physiotherapy students, who seemed to have an insatiable desire to learn. 'They're so keen!' he would say to me most afternoons, as if the more he said it, the more he would fathom it.

One afternoon in April, he told me about the lectures that he had given that morning on the anatomy of the spinal column. Apparently, the ten second-year students had sat quietly on their stools while they diligently copied down notes from the whiteboard. Then they had taken it in turns to place masking tape on the skeleton to symbolise each muscle group. While they were taking turns with the masking tape Darren looked around the group and noticed that Ajit, an earnest young man from the south of Nepal, had smeared his whole forehead in red *tika*. *Tika* is a bright red mixture usually made from rice and food colouring and Hindu Nepalis place it on their foreheads to indicate that the gods have been worshipped and sacrifices given, a process known as *puja*.

Although *tika* is a common sight in Nepal, Darren was sure that his students at DMI didn't normally come to lectures with their foreheads so completely covered. So he turned to Ajit as he settled back in his seat and said, 'Have you been doing *puja*?'

'Yes I have,' Ajit smiled up at Darren, 'to the god who gives a good education.'

'Oh,' said Darren, smiling to himself, 'and am I not giving you a good education?'

Ajit assured him that he was doing very well; the *puja* was just a backup.

By the end of April we decided that it was my turn to lecture the physio students for a week. Prior to leaving Australia, we had come to an agreement with INF and DMI that as a couple we would be able to job-share the tutoring role. I'm sure that it sounded good in Australia, but that morning as I made my way out our front door in Dhulikhel, laden down with text books and Nepali phrases buzzing in my brain, I could only look back at the boys and wish that I hadn't been quite so committed to equity.

For the whole way down our hill and past the post office, the football field and the prison, I wished that I hadn't agreed to it. I was so busy worrying about it that I hardly saw the man walking ahead of me struggling under a load of bricks. I was so busy worrying that I hardly noticed the children running alongside me with their old bike tyres attached to long pieces of wire. I didn't even call out my *namaste* to Bagmati. I was just too busy worrying. In Australia, my physio experience was all tied up with amputee and stroke rehabilitation. In Nepal in the nineties I had drawn from that experience as I worked at the INF-run leprosy hospital. But now, ten years on, it all seemed out of date or irrelevant. What if I could no longer apply amputee rehabilitation to the Nepali context? What if I couldn't answer their questions? Or, even more frighteningly, what if they didn't understand a word I said?

The DMI building is a large white structure sitting squarely in the paddy fields behind Dhulikhel hospital. To reach it you have to walk through the hospital, past the medical wards and the laboratory and then down 93 stone steps that lead to its fairly grand entrance. That morning I slipped in quietly trying not to listen to the echo of my steps in the hall and then I made my way to the physio teaching room. Subarna, apparently one of our keenest students, was already there filling up bottles of water from the filter by the door.

'Good morning, ma'am,' she said, bowing in my direction.

I smiled at her and vaguely wondered what the correct response might be from a lecturer in a Nepali institute. I had never been called ma'am before. While I was wondering and sorting out my lecture notes, another eight students came to the door. Each one stopped at the door, bowed very politely and said, 'May I come in, ma'am?'

'Yes,' I said, eight times, still wondering.

Then the last student arrived in a mad hurry, looking at his watch and wiping his feet all in one go. His words tumbled out much faster than the previous eight. 'May I come in, ma'am?'

I glanced at the clock and realised why he was so worried. It was five minutes past nine. Apparently, at DMI, if a student is five minutes late the door is locked and the student is barred from entry. 'Yes,' I said again smiling, deciding to err on the side of grace on my first day of work.

For the next four hours I introduced the concept of amputee rehabilitation. The students sat quietly and copied down notes, then answered my questions slowly and thoughtfully. It was all going very well and I was up to the section where I planned to cover the causes of amputation. So I told them that there were five main causes of amputation and I began writing the numbers 1 to 5 on the whiteboard. Then I turned around and asked them if they could guess what those five causes might be.

'Bombs,' said Hom.

'Gunfire,' said Ajit.

'Grenades,' said Binayak.

'Landslides,' said Subarna.

'Leprosy,' said Prathana.

I wrote them all down on the board as they spoke them and then looked back at their list. In the pause that followed, I looked down at the list in my notes, which had been written in the West by Western practitioners, for Western students. My list read: peripheral vascular disease (gangrene due to diabetes and smoking), infection, cancer, trauma and congenital deformities. My list included percentages and statistics, numbers that could be verified and quoted in medical journals. In contrast, their list seemed somehow more real, speaking the stories of a country at war. It was another gentle reminder that I was living in a country not my own, where nothing can be assumed and very little can be prescribed. I gave the students a ten-minute break and sat staring out at the paddy fields. Perhaps, instead of me fretting about applying amputee rehabilitation to the Nepali context, the students would do a perfectly thorough job themselves.

And so they did, for the rest of that week. We made pretend patients from old stockings and dressed them in Darren's shorts before practising our bandaging techniques on their compliant stumps. We pretended to perform hundreds of exercises and stretches on these limp, but helpful, beings. Then we carried the stockinged people through the bazaar and all the way home to the stares of the passers-by. On the very last day the students and I took the local bus to the nearest prosthetic facility where they were able to ask their remaining questions to the very experienced man in charge. I stood to the side listening to their questions and feeling the pride within me – that somehow in this context they had learnt something. And then the next week, we celebrated. All the students came over to our house for a festive chicken *dal bhat* which was to farewell Gillian, our Canadian fellow tutor, who was going home on leave. It was a balmy evening in Dhulikhel and the cricket match was hotly contested outside, while inside the music played and the food kept coming. Later in the evening, I sat on one of our bamboo stools and watched the students laugh as they wrapped themselves in saris and batted balloons in the air. And as I sat there smiling, I thought to myself about the concept of belonging. It struck me, as the balloons danced wildly before my eyes, that maybe the degree to which I belong anywhere isn't actually measurable. Maybe it's just a gentle, onward movement. Maybe it's just a sense or a feeling that I have towards a place and a people that tells me, through an accumulation of moments, that I'm home. And that evening, amidst the smell of *dal bhat* and the shouts in Nepali, I felt that I was.

Darren, of course, when the evening was over, wanted to know when I would be teaching my next block of physiotherapy to the students. He even had the calendar out and the red pen, ready to colour in some time that would signal a break and a change of pace for him. But I cleverly evaded his questions and said that we should think about it for a few days. And in those few days, as so often happens, everything changed.

By then, it was the first week in May and Stephen had completed nearly four months of schooling at KUPS. While Darren and I had been teaching and preparing, planting and praying, Stephen's days had begun with a run down our hill in time for the bus and then a creaky journey through the Dhulikhel bazaar and around the next mountain until the bus reached the plateau on the very top. On the very top of the mountain sat the school – a rectangle of brick buildings facing the tallest mountains in the world. The two hundred children piled out from the buses and began their day's work with assembly and an extended Hindu meditation. They then worked on maths and English before breaking for *dal bhat* at half past ten in the big mess hall and *khaja* (snacks) at 2 p.m. The long day would finish with the return bus trip home and a much slower walk up our hill.

During Stephen's first few weeks at KUPS, I made the journey with him quite a few times. I watched him, nervously, as he located his classroom and a boy that he vaguely recognised. I felt the shudders within me as he stood there silently, waiting and watching. I listened to the chant of the meditation and it felt like a steam train rolling down the hill, gaining pace and rhythm as it went. I watched his retreating 8-year-old back as he was swallowed up by the classroom and then I went to drink the obligatory cup of *chiya* with the principal.

I worried.

For the first few months, it all seemed to be going quite well. Stephen learnt a whole lot of Nepali history and geography and could quote the names of Nepali kings that I had never heard of – not to mention the seventy-five Nepali geographical districts. He made friends with two Nepali boys – Santosh and Sujay and he would tell me how much *dal bhat* they ate during break time. In art, he did a project on Mahatma Ghandi and was commended for the best drawing in the class.

Then, one day in April, he came to me after school and said, 'Now, I know it's true.'

'What's true?' I said, not really concentrating.

'I know that what we believe is true.' I put down the washing and gave him my full attention.

'And how is it that you know?'

He paused before he put it into words. He'd been thinking a great deal. 'I've seen what they do. I've seen what they have to do – every morning. They have to kneel down in front of those frightening statues in the temples every morning. The statues aren't even real, they're made of concrete. The kids are scared, but they're forced to do it. They have to do it.' He looked at me, and slowed down his words. 'We don't believe in gods made of concrete. We believe in the living God, and I believe – that he loves me.'

I thought about his words before I replied. 'I suppose, before we came to Nepal, you knew about the living God, but you didn't know, you hadn't seen the other options.'

'That's right! But now I have seen them, and now I'm sure.'

Later on that evening, I found him tucked up in his bed and staring out at the Himalayas with his Bible opened on his lap at Psalm 121. His lips were moving noiselessly and his gaze was shifting back and forth from the window to the Bible on his lap. I crept back out and then rejoined him later.

'You've been reading the Psalms?' I said.

'Not really, just number 121,' he said as his finger moved down the page. 'I like it and I'm memorising it so that I can say it in my head when everybody else does their Hindu meditation.'

We read it together:

> I lift up my eyes to the hills –
> where does my help come from?
> My help comes from the LORD,
> the Maker of heaven and earth.
> He will not let your foot slip –
> he who watches over you will not slumber;
> indeed, he who watches over Israel
> will neither slumber nor sleep.
> The LORD watches over you –
> the LORD is your shade at your right hand;
> the sun will not harm you by day,

nor the moon by night.
The LORD will keep you from all harm –
he will watch over your life;
the LORD will watch over your coming and going
both now and for evermore.

I quietly wiped tears from my eyes. He who watches over me
also watches over our 8-year-old son. He who neither slum-
bers nor sleeps has his hand on our son. In the middle of a
very strict Hindu school, in the middle of Hindu meditations,
the Maker of heaven and earth teaches him truths that he can't
learn anywhere else. He gives our son the treasures of darkness, riches stored in secret places, so that he will know that he
is the Lord.

Towards the end of April, all the children at KUPS did
extensive exams. Even the revising was extensive.
Occasionally, if a child didn't know the answer to the question,
an arm was raised in physical punishment. The arm landed as
a slap across the face. Stephen would come home with stories
of punishment and with the fear that it would happen to him.
He would also come home with two hours of homework each
night and the fear of punishment if it wasn't completed. One
night he admitted to us that he was so worried about the punishment that he wasn't sleeping at night. He also appeared to
be retreating into himself, becoming more and more isolated
by the language barrier and the worldview differences.
Although the classes were in English, the children spoke in
Nepali socially and in the break times. Stephen, not comfortable with using his Nepali, seemed to be becoming an obser-
ver of life at school rather than a participant.

I talked about it with Darren after Stephen had gone to bed
that night. The reason that we had encouraged him to try
Nepali school was to give him the social contacts that we
thought would be good for him. We thought that a positive

time in another culture involved making friends from that culture and we thought that attending a local school would be the best place for Stephen to do that. The thoughts were good, we acknowledged late that night, but we also acknowledged that it wasn't working. For me, the hardest thing was to realise that it was OK to make a decision and then, some months later, go back on that very decision; in fact, to turn around and do the exact opposite. But the more we talked about it that night, the more we realised that we needed to pull Stephen out of Nepali school and begin home-school. Indeed, it seemed so clear to us, that we didn't even need a timeline or a plan of action. We would simply begin the very next day. So in the morning, the first thing we did was to tell Stephen.

He was thrilled. Darren took him for an early morning bike ride down the road that led from Dhulikhel out to Tibet and by the time they returned, he was buzzing with the excitement of doing school at home. He couldn't wait. He even found the maths and English workbooks and sorted out his desk upstairs before I finished my breakfast. It was 3 May and he was all set to begin.

He was all set, but for me, moving from the decision to do home-school and then actually carrying it out took slightly more than half an hour. I had always thought that home-school might be something we would need to do – hence the workbooks – but I had no real plan as to how I would actually do it. Not being a teacher, I had no idea what it entailed or even what subjects I needed to cover. I didn't know what an 8-year-old living in Australia normally covered in history and geography, science and social studies, let alone what we, living in Nepal, should try to replicate. The only thing that was clear to me was that we should begin – and so we did. I finished my porridge and put the bread on and then Stephen and I found our way through a few pages of the maths and English workbooks. Chris and Jeremy found their way through a whole box of Duplo in the next room and then we all found the softest patch of grass below the plum trees and stared up at the clouds, eating peanuts and talking about what we should do next.

'How about we study every country in the whole world?' suggested Stephen.

I smiled. 'That's a good idea – but where should we start?'

'South America,' he said, and then cried out as a scarlet-breasted sunbird landed on the banana tree behind us. I turned around and the flash of gold came to life and disappeared into John and Margaret's garden.

'Right – South America it is!' I said.

So over the next few weeks we pored over pictures of the Amazon rainforest and became enchanted by the giant leeches and other strange creatures that seemed to inhabit the largest jungle in the world. Stephen drew pictures of the Andes mountains and spent hours staring at detailed maps of the only two landlocked countries in South America – Bolivia and Paraguay. Then we tried to imagine living by the Amazon river in a constant temperature of 27 ° Celsius.

'Imagine never having winter clothes or summer clothes!' said Stephen.

'Imagine it!' I replied.

While we were busy imagining another strange and wonderful continent, the temperature around us, in our own landlocked country, grew steadily higher. In mid-June the monsoon arrived and our crisp Himalayan mornings gave way to thick fog and torrential downpours. The range of mountains that we saw from our bedroom window disappeared into a swirling grey mass of cloud and our terraces came alive with the kind of growth that felt like it was going to follow me back into the living room.

Srijana, who had never cooked on anything but an open fire, seemed to know exactly what to plant in our terraces and she knew exactly when to plant it. Not only did she know what and when to plant, she cheerfully went ahead and did it. As we watched our garden transform into a green oasis, the reality of life in front of us pushed our imaginings to the side and we moved into a unit on 'living things' in science.

On one particularly wet morning we sat on the back porch growing ever deafer as the rain thundered down all around us and it seemed that we could actually see the corn growing.

'It's taller than me!' yelled Chris, almost skidding on the steps in his excitement.

They all slipped their *chappals* on and raced down to the first terrace, laughing as they sloshed about beneath the corn and finding strange slugs and brightly-coloured bugs. Then they came in from the mud and the rain and we all settled back down at the table to inspect the living things that they'd collected. We were just drawing pictures of the red-backed beetle when Jeremy screamed, 'Aghhh, Mum! A leech!'

We all looked down at Jeremy's foot which was swinging madly beneath the table. Hanging on from its suckers was an enormous bulge of black leech. It looked almost as long as it was wide and bulbous. Stephen ran for the salt and together they disembowelled it. Blood spurted out all over the thin carpet and four pairs of eyes watched its last throes of life. Then they all stared as its body lay still, curled up and silent.

'I think that's a dead thing,' said Stephen.

We then moved on to definitions of the living and the dead, having already witnessed both phases.

To increase our knowledge of living things during that monsoon, we began a collection of tadpoles and guinea pigs, tiny chicks and ducklings, hens and roosters. The first to arrive in the household were two fluffy baby chicks. We found them for sale in a cardboard box in the bazaar and we couldn't immediately think of a reason why we shouldn't buy them. So they made the journey back home on the front of Stephen's bicycle and then spent the rest of the day in various positions attached to the boys. Chris tucked his yellow ball of fluff into his shirt front and pronounced that it was to be named Jacki. Unfortunately, and within seconds, Jeremy also called his Jacki. It's the bane of Chris's life, the way Jeremy copies him. So, he turned around and said that his was no longer Jacki, it was Chuck Chuck.

The guinea pigs came from Kathmandu and were easily named Scamp and Scurry. They were the first of their kind ever seen in Dhulikhel. Our Nepali friends lined up at the door just to see these strange creatures. They would pick them up and turn them over and then discuss it between themselves, differing only over whether the guinea pigs were actually very big rats or very small rabbits. Bagmati's daughter was firmly in the 'small rabbit' camp. She would even call her friends to come and see the strange small rabbits. If anyone complained about the size of their hind legs, she would merely reply, 'They haven't grown yet.'

But the question remained some months later, 'So . . . why are its feet *still* small?'

We discovered that you can do applied learning anywhere. After the monsoon finished, we took an excursion down to the national park in the south of Nepal and went riding on elephants, hunting for wild things. Our elephant, which Jeremy had named, all by himself, 'Aeroplane', moved noiselessly through the jungle and we learnt about the strength of its trunk. To our astonished eyes, Aeroplane wrapped its trunk around trees in our path and ripped them straight out of the ground, tossing them aside in the same way that we toss banana skins. We sat swaying on its back, feeling its rhythm and learning how to spot herds of rhinoceros through the dense jungle.

Then, on another excursion, we trekked the Annapurnas and the boys rode donkeys through the deepest valley in the world. They found fossils in the river bed and ate Tibetan bread for breakfast. Yet another time, we journeyed to the Tibetan border and watched the monkeys in China. We laughed as they gambolled at the base of the waterfall. We would have stayed longer on that particular excursion, but we were also learning something about Chinese soldiers – that they stand very straight and jealously guard their border.

In between excursions we built tree houses and soccer terraces in the extensive back garden. We learnt how to make plum jam and ate it until it was coming out of our ears. Srijana taught us how to grow corn and beans and peas and garlic and spinach. Then the banana tree surprised us all by actually producing the most enormous bunch of bananas. We kept a close eye on it, awaiting the great day when they would all be edible. But in that particular month of home-school, the learning outcome was singular: no matter how carefully you watch a bunch of bananas, they will all ripen while your backs are turned. In one magical moment all one hundred of them turned from hard and green to an oozing mass of yellow and black. It was simply amazing. Even the monkey didn't want them.

In all, the first few months of home-school were as exciting for me as they were for the boys. I was keen to learn and to try out all my new ideas and it even felt quite freeing. No longer being bound by school hours or terms or holidays meant that we could come and go as we pleased. As well as the excursions it meant that we could spend more time with an Irish family who lived on the other side of Dhulikhel and who also home-schooled three of their four children. Avril and I shared resources and inspiration as well as lots of cups of well-brewed tea. She pointed me to a library in Kathmandu where I even found books on home-schooling. I would wake up early and read them first thing in the morning, just to get me in the mood. Even when a lesson itself didn't turn out as well as I'd hoped, there was always the next day. There was always a fresh idea or a new tack to take that would, of course, transform the whole thing – into what it was meant to be. Some days, while we transformed, we even forgot about the war. But that was only on the days that we stayed inside.

4

HE STANDS THERE WITH US

Outside, it was impossible to forget. Whenever we walked along the ridge from our house to the Dhulikhel bazaar, we were not only joined by women and their *dokos*, milkmen and their milk cans and children and their clipboards but also by soldiers and their machine-guns. They were careering past in jeeps. They were settled behind their mounds of sandbags. They were manning lookouts. They were training their rifles on every passer-by – armed, ready and awaiting the events of the day.

Since 1996, the Maoists had been fighting a civil war in Nepal that had been getting increasingly bloodthirsty as the years went by and their demands weren't met by the government. By the time we returned to Nepal in October 2003, 10,000 people had lost their lives in the conflict. Riots, bombs and blockades were common. For us, it was a very new aspect of Nepali life and it was very unsettling. Nepal in the early nineties had been a land of unshakeable poverty and political instability, yet it had also been primarily a land of peace, a land where we didn't question our personal safety and where we were not woken from our sleep by the sound of bombs.

But by 2003, the contrasts were evident. From the Kathmandu airport onwards there was an ever-growing number of soldiers settled in groups and keeping a firm eye on the proceedings. Their fingers were on the triggers. They gathered in groups at regular checkpoints on every road. They sat in the rear of open-backed jeeps, their rifles angled in every direction.

In unmistakable blue and green uniforms they were easily recognisable. But who was on the other side? Who were the targets? It was a difficult question. Occupying 80 per cent of the rural country, the Maoists based themselves in the more remote hill villages. They, of course, didn't wear recognisable anything.

As well as the changes on the street, the changes within the country seemed to be in the people themselves. As we sat in taxis and then chatted to the shopkeepers, we sensed a new era of hopelessness. Every taxi driver was worried about his nation and his people. Every shopkeeper was worried about the loss of life, the displaced people and the economic downturn. They let their worry seep out in their words and in their sighs, until it hung about them like clouds of pessimism. They could see no way forward out of the political stalemate. They were depressed and cautious. A level of suspicion had crept into relationships that were previously trusted. If nobody knew who the targets were, how could anyone stay well clear of them?

Quite early on, we went to visit some Nepali friends that we had known in the nineties. We were just settling down to our second helping of *dal bhat* when there was a knock at the door. It broke the silence. We all looked up and I watched as a frown passed over the face of our host. He went to the door and opened it carefully.

Over the threshold stepped a well-dressed stranger carrying a small rucksack.

'Can I stay the night?' the stranger asked our host in Nepali. 'I'm from your village and I'm a friend of one of your friends.'

Our friend looked at his feet. He hesitated, he asked some questions and he began fidgeting in the manner of one feeling embarrassed. Ordinarily, this lovely Christian family would have invited him in, shared a meal with him and given him a bed. After all, someone from your own village and a friend of a close friend was as good as family.

This family also house four orphans and have fourteen extended family members in their house. They are generous. But on that night, the response was guarded and after some time spent chatting, our host reluctantly made his decision.

'I'm sorry, but you'll have to move on.'

The family stood back as the young man turned and headed off into the night. Our host then turned to us, wanting to find words for the feelings within him. '*Ke garne?*' he looked terribly troubled. 'What can I do? How can I know? Whom can I trust?' His questions tumbled out like a pack of cards. 'These days, we're all suspicious; we're all torn in our hearts. We just don't know what to do. We don't know if they are friends or army or Maoists. We don't know if our lives will be threatened if we invite them in, or worse, if we'll be threatened if we don't invite them in. As Christians, are we not to love others? Are we not to care for them and feed them? Are we not to give them clothes and a bed? But how can I do that and at the same time risk the lives of my own family? What can I do?'

The heart of Nepali culture is to extend hospitality to their own people. They have always been more than generous with their homes and their food. But by 2003, the political situation had made it increasingly difficult. The history of violence had robbed many of their trust. They were torn by their own questions and left without answers. If *they* were torn and confused by the questions, how could we, as inexperienced *bideshis* even begin to understand the complexities of the new situation? How could we begin to understand the cues? How could we begin to fathom what we should do and what we should be worried about?

At first I looked to the locals for their reactions. Some of the women on the street in Dhulikhel seemed to be carrying on as normal. They were collecting water at the tap and carrying their *dokos* through the bazaar. The children were playing with their *chungis* (balls made of rubber bands) right in front of the army camp, seemingly unaware that a heavily armed soldier had his gun trained on their backs. But then, in the middle of my questions, I looked closer and realised that there was much more to it. The reason that they carried on normally was because they had no choice. They still needed water and they still needed grass, in order to live. The children still needed to play, somehow.

Every morning and evening about thirty soldiers in rows of blue and green would run through the town of Dhulikhel. The noise would escalate. They would thunder past in neat rows, their boots clanging on the cobbled pavements and then sloshing in the mud. That was the time to get out of the way or be trampled underfoot. Another place to show respect was at all the checkpoints that dotted the main roads. These were each manned by at least a dozen well-armed soldiers. Local buses would stop and all the passengers would disembark in order to file solemnly through the checkpoint. Bags and names were checked and permission was granted to carry on. I would sit there with the boys and watch the faces of those around me for a response. I would wait for signs of irritation at the time-consuming inconvenience. I would wait for something mirroring my own frustration. But they didn't show it, they just walked. The *bideshis* were usually waved quietly through, another reminder that it was not our war. Another reminder that we were separate and distinct, not rooted in this land as everybody else was.

Our house in Dhulikhel sat halfway up a forested hill, but only about 100 metres down the hill was the army camp. The sounds of their practise would echo across the valley and thunder into our living area. We would startle, catch each other's eye and ask ourselves the questions. Is it just practise or is it something more serious? We knew what we were listening for. We'd trained our ears. Is the gunfire regular? Is there a pattern to it? Is there a sound like a response? Is there answering gunfire? The questions were easy to answer in the daytime. In the daytime if we were worried we could merely position ourselves somewhere near a window where we could watch a neighbour. If the neighbour looked unconcerned then we went back to school. But if we were worried at night-time, it was much more off-putting. There was nobody to see. There were no clues as to where the sounds were coming from. There was only the darkness.

I struggled the most with how much to tell the boys. I wanted to find that fine line that would prepare them well in the event of an emergency but not scare them to death. I didn't even know whether the fine line existed.

Stephen soon became particularly skilled at assessing gunfire. He could easily figure out whether it sounded like his game of darts or not and then he would let me know, 'They're just practising, Mum.' And we would all carry on with what we were doing.

Another morning Chris passed me in the kitchen on his way up the stairs, 'Mummy, hundreds of army men just came running down our hill.' He stopped to look at me. 'But they didn't shoot us.' And then he carried on upstairs while his words rang in my ears. At first, his tone of voice had seemed as ordinary as the gecko behind the curtain or the monkey on the roof. But then, was it really? What brought on the qualifier? How do we, as parents, ever really know what's in the minds of our children?

During our first year in Dhulikhel the Maoists would call a *bandh* at least once a week. It was a technique to put pressure on the government but it took a long time to get my head around it. The *bandh* was a strike which was either a transport *bandh* (no vehicles allowed on the roads) an educational *bandh* (no schools or universities allowed to open) or a full *bandh* (no vehicles, no shops, no trading, no schools, no universities, nothing much at all). The *bandh* could then be either localised to a certain area or district or it could be a nationwide *bandh*. Either way, it was usually followed to the letter. There had been too many stories of shops destroyed and cars blown up by Maoists for the people not to obey the terms. The strangest thing was the way that these *bandhs* were communicated and then enforced. Nobody ever seemed to know till the actual day if there was one and then it was mostly word of mouth that leaked out the possibilities. At our house we learnt a new morning greeting, 'Is there a *bandh* today?' And then some clarity, 'What sort of *bandh*?'

Then began the stranger process of trying to figure out how that might impact our day. The questions were numerous. Can I buy bananas? Should Darren go to work? Will the students be there? Will I bother ironing anything? Will the buses be running? Can I get into Kathmandu? Or even worse – can we go on holidays? That was during our first Easter when we were trying to do a week's trekking in the Annapurnas. We ended up beginning the trek right at our own front door – a transport *bandh* meant that we walked for two hours to get to the nearest operating bus.

For me, who treats planning as a hobby, it was tough. Never knowing what tomorrow would bring, how could I make a plan? When could I go to Kathmandu for shopping or banking? What if we run out of money? When could I expect to send or receive mail? How could we pick up our visitors from overseas? When would the vehicles start running again? The questions were numerous and the answer was always the same. I have no idea.

In previous chapters of my life when one area of life was out of control, I could usually count on the mundane to be still ticking over. When Darren was in hospital having major heart operations, the supermarket still sold bread and the roads were still open. When we longed for another child, the postman still came and the credit card still worked. It was an entirely new thing for the mundane to be threatened. When the mundane is threatened, it feels a bit like you're trying to eat a three-course meal off a plate which is not there. The meal is good, but the plate is critical. Without the plate, the meal hangs suspended in nothing. Shall I put it in my mouth? Or not?

Sometimes, it was easy for us to retreat into the safe world within our home. We would sit on the back porch and play with the guinea pigs or check on the tadpoles. We would even retreat further by studying the major towns in South America. We would still read the daily newspapers but we would keep them at arm's length in order to keep functioning. Both the *Kathmandu Post* and the *Himalayan* were delivered to our door at breakfast time. The headlines were consistently and predictably disastrous. We would glance at them while we monitored the bowls of porridge and sticky Horlicks. We would read the fine print while restraining the boys as they argued over favourite spoons. A dozen Maoists killed, protests in Kathmandu over the capture of student leaders, rumours of atrocities by the army against women, children involved in the planting of landmines. It was an extremely sombre way to begin the day. It was so sombre that we tried not to face it. We tried to think of something else and gain distance where there was none.

One day, Darren went on a motorbike trip into the surrounding hills to attempt to find a patient's relative. He didn't find the relative. Instead, he found a village which had been overtaken by Maoists. In order to keep their homes the villagers had to come up with one million rupees (about £9,000). Simple villagers do not have one million rupees, they don't even have enough to buy three tomatoes. Schools had been closed down, young men conscripted, businesses had gone bust and fields were lying empty. Then, while Darren was asking for directions to the patient's house, along came the Maoists themselves. Darren was told to leave the area or he would be kidnapped. Not one to deliberate over such decisions, he left!

It was a timely reminder to us that the strife lay around us and amidst us. We could not and we should not pretend distance. Somehow we needed to see the land of Nepal through God's eyes. Not through our own eyes or the media's eyes but through the eyes of God, the one who set the heavens in place and laid the foundations of the earth. The Lord our maker cares about the stories behind the news headlines. He doesn't need to read them – he already knows them and somehow, beyond our imaginings, he holds them.

In his book, *He Still Moves Stones*, Max Lucado wrote of a carving found on the wall of a concentration camp. On it, a prisoner had inscribed these words:

> I believe in the sun, even when it doesn't shine.
> I believe in love, even when it isn't shown.
> I believe in God, even when he doesn't speak.

During the conflict in Nepal, where we saw at a daily level the horrors of war, we needed to learn to see with eyes that saw the unseen. We needed eyes that saw the sovereignty of God, yet still joined with hands that weren't afraid to touch the pain. We needed bodies that would not give in to distance.

In August 2004, after we'd been in Dhulikhel for seven months, we awoke to news that the Maoists had announced a siege of Kathmandu and would be blockading the city for an indefinite time period. That meant that all of the roads coming in and out of the city were blocked and no trucks or goods were allowed through. There are really only two main roads in and out of the capital. There is the road that winds through

Dhulikhel and ends up in Tibet and there is the road to Pokhara that connects Kathmandu not only to the rest of the country but also to the Indian border. Both roads were closed. Prices immediately skyrocketed in the capital, with tomatoes going up to 200 rupees a kilogram, ten times their normal price. People on the streets and in the little shops were talking about how much gas they had left to cook on. The petrol man in Dhulikhel said that he had run out of petrol and was unsure whether he would be getting any more. We sat in our closest shop and listened to the concerns of our *sahuji*. If the roads didn't open up, there would be no more goods. There would be nothing to sell. We worried and we tuned into the news. We sat in our kitchen hunched over the shortwave radio and we heard the reporters predict that the blockade could last a month or more. I looked about me and thought about our food supplies. Even more alarmingly, I tried to imagine not being able to leave the town for an indefinite time period. But what about . . . ?

During that week I sat on our back porch every afternoon and considered the situation in front of me. I thought of the despair as businesses folded and family members went hungry. I thought of the woman at church whose son had been kidnapped by Maoists. I thought of Hom, our physio student whose house had been bombed by Maoists. None of the family members had been hurt but their buffalo had died – their only livelihood. I thought of the morning's paper that had reported that Nepal was a nation tumbling to the brink of anarchy. I thought of the victims of the conflict who arrived at Dhulikhel hospital every day. And then I thought very slowly of the words of the prisoner in the concentration camp, 'I believe in God, even when he doesn't speak.'

I repeated the words over and over in my head, one after the other, until slowly I began to hope again. I began to hope in God, who does not always speak, but who takes us to the edge of a problem and stands there with us.

5

BE READY TO GO

By September the road had opened up again and one Friday we took the local bus to Kathmandu and revelled in the sights and sounds of the big city. It was still raining though and the two-hour journey took us straight through a monsoonal downpour. The boys and I were squashed into the back seat of the bus while Darren was somewhere outside riding his bike. Inside the bus, the Hindi dance music blared out from the overworked speakers. 'Bop ee dah, Bop ee dah, Bop ee dah, Bop ee do.' Five heavily decorated Hindu gods stared in at us from the side windows of the bus: their faces fixed, their eyes unseeing.

The boys and I stared out of the streaming windows at the flooded landscape and I thought about the way we each see things differently. If you had asked Stephen he would have told you about the bicycles that sprayed water as they rode through the flooded streets. He would have told you about the water that poured into the little shops down the street. If you had asked Chris, he would have told you about the lights on the aeroplanes as they negotiated the black clouds. Then he would have told you about how wet the soldiers seemed to be getting. If you had asked Jeremy, he would have told you about the buffalo in the mud and the other strange objects that were floating down the street; buckets and pieces of fruit and bits of clothing, all bobbing up and down as the waves sent them in new and exciting directions. While the boys were staring at the rivers all around us, I watched the way an occasional gleam of light reflected off my neighbour's bangles. Then I watched the Bagmati River swell and burst its banks. The water rode in waves straight into the tents of the squatters by the river.

Later, Darren told us about his bicycle ride. He told us about the pot-holes and the mud puddles and the way he had veered to avoid them. He told us about the cows on the road and the way the taxis had swerved and the trucks overtaken him. He had noticed the people who were on the road and he had deftly avoided them, keeping his eye on the route up ahead.

We seem to live in the same world but see it differently. The ways that we perceive our world then become the very heart of us, the language that we use to make sense of the things that we see. Sometimes, very occasionally, we need to check out the way that others see things – just in case we have missed something vital.

We did this regularly with the security situation. Once a month, the INF security team would send out an email to all INF members updating us on the current political turmoil. Each email would cover basic information regarding what had happened across the country during that month: *bandhs*, road closures, attacks and curfews. Then there would be a section where the information was interpreted and understood in the light of what could possibly happen next. And then finally, there was advice. We would always read that section very carefully. 'Listen to your local radio.' 'Avoid the places in your area that are known to be flash points.' 'Re-read the section entitled "hibernation" in your INF personal security manual.' 'Check that your go-bag is appropriately stocked.' The advice changed every month but almost always there was a reminder to have our 'go-bag' ready and appropriately stocked. It was a reminder that we were living in a situation of political tension and that we must be ready to go at a moment's notice, whenever the signal was given, with our go-bag ready and waiting by the door.

Our go-bag, when properly stocked, was enormous. It was much too enormous to leave by the front door, so instead we stuffed it into the bottom section of the cupboard in our room. It was even too big for the cupboard and the extra bulges would leak out every day, reminding us of its presence. To circumnavigate our bed each night, we had to give the go-bag a shove and then quickly try and close the cupboard doors, before it all fell out again and blocked our way around the bed.

But that was during the initial months of enthusiasm. Slowly, but surely, the go-bag decreased in size. Initially and optimistically, I had worked my way down the suggested list in the INF personal security manual and packed into the bag a change of clothes for everyone (summer and winter because we could never be sure which season we would have to race out the door), toiletries and a first aid kit, enough water and food to get us to India (which would be a good 100 kilometre walk – can you imagine how much the boys would need to eat!), our passports and official documents, even notebooks and matches, torches and candles, sewing kits and pocket knives. No wonder it didn't fit in the cupboard!

But then, after the initial few months, Stephen began to outgrow his tracksuit trousers and complain about the chill at his ankles. We replaced them from the go-bag. Then, Jeremy chewed up his toothbrush and presented it as a fuzzy stick one winter's evening. We replaced it from the go-bag. Not long after that, Chris's birthday arrived and we remembered that we had hidden a fantastic bag of sweets in the go-bag. They came out and were enjoyed by everyone. By the time we had been in Dhulikhel for nine months, the go-bag was hardly a problem at all. We had used up most of its bulges and we could easily circumnavigate it at night.

I would rationalise it to myself as I read the fine print in the monthly security emails. I would stare at the screen and tell myself happily that it was all about preparedness. If I was prepared to go, then that was the main thing. Instead of considering our diminishing go-bag, I would look around me and take a little bit of pride in the way I ran my house. I knew where everything was. If I ever needed anything, I could always find it within moments. If we really needed to evacuate in a hurry, I would be able to do it as quickly as anyone. It would surely only take me half an hour to find the things that we would need. After all, I was the queen of packing.

I could rationalise the go-bag issue but being *ready to go* was a phrase that it took me years to fit within the spaces of my mind. If I was really ready to go, why was I planting another crop of corn? If I was really ready to go, why was I planning the next year's home-school topics? If I was really ready to go, why was I putting so much energy into the relationships that surrounded me?

I decided during that first year that it was almost impossible to do both, to plant deeply and, at the same time, to be ready to go. At first I thought that I could keep one foot here and still have my eyes over there. But, after a while I realised that it was impossible. Instead, I could only do one thing at a time. Perhaps it was a bit like when I was a kid and trying to pat my head and rub my stomach at the same time. It would always begin well as I showed off my trick to the admiring relatives but sooner or later, the hand on my head would be rubbing my hair into a fuzzy ball of static. And at that point, I would give in and acknowledge the drive within my hands to engage in the same task. I would recognise that I hadn't been designed to do two opposing things in the one moment. And in Dhulikhel I realised that I hadn't been designed to plant deeply while being ready to go.

By the time the monsoon of 2004 finished, we were well and truly planted. We were not holding lightly and we were not ready to go. Darren had nearly taught a whole year of his anatomy and clinical assessment subjects at DMI. He had written all of his lectures and was revelling in being able to turn up to the classroom without having done hours and hours of preparation. Instead of late nights at the computer, he was enjoying the relationships that he had with the students and the impromptu gatherings over *dal bhat*. He was enjoying their laughter over new ways to describe muscle spasm and their attempts to add cricket terms to their physio vocabulary. He was well planted and doing what he had always wanted to be doing – training Nepali physiotherapists for the future.

But it was not only at work that he was well-planted. In our Nepali church he'd quickly become involved in a Bible study group of mostly young men. They would meet on Wednesday afternoons after work and our living area would fill with the sounds of Nepali conversation as they tried hard to apply God's word. By the time the monsoon was over, they were so comfortable, that they would wander into the kitchen before and after the study in order to laugh with the boys. The boys laughed back.

Then, for Darren, there were the hours outside of work and church and family. He had, by chance, met Suman, an ex-national cyclist who introduced him to hundreds of mountain bike trails around the hills and valleys of Dhulikhel. They would get up in the early hours, even before the milkman arrived, in order to explore the rises and falls of altitude before work. While he stared out over the terraces and caught sight of a new trail, he was not preparing to leave. He was planting.

Being deeply planted meant that we were putting all of our energy into the people and the life around us. We were still reading and writing emails to our friends back in the other land, but when anything happened to make us smile or cry or worry, the very first people that we went to were the ones in front of us, the ones who were physically present – not the ones who existed in that other, virtual world. It was a good way to be.

Along with Darren, I was also feeling that I had re-orientated my world. I felt like I had formed the kind of friendships that I could turn to when I needed to share my inner life. I would spend time with Srijana outside her mud hut or I would grab some moments with Saru, the pastor's wife, as she sat in their little paper shop in the bazaar. On Wednesday mornings, I would walk with Gillian and on Tuesday afternoons, I would share stories with Avril, our Irish friend who lived across the paddy fields. On other quieter afternoons, I would pop in next door and eat Anzac biscuits with Margaret as she relaxed after work.

We were planting deeply together and sharing the life that we lived – together. But even as we planted, once a month we would sit in front of the computer and read the security email. It would remind us that the life we were living, the life in front of us, was not all that there was. We might have to leave and we might have to leave in a hurry. So, we must be ready; we must check the go-bag.

How could we do that? How could we hold the two together? How could we plant deeply and at the same time keep our go-bag well-stocked and our feet ready to run out of the door? One afternoon as I considered the impossible nature of the questions, I began to catch a glimpse of something new. And it was this: if I could somehow learn to plant deeply in Nepal and keep my eyes on Australia, then perhaps I could also learn to plant deeply on this earth and keep my eyes on heaven. That afternoon I had also been reading Paul's letter to the Corinthians, 'So we fix our eyes not on what is seen, but on what is unseen. For what is seen is temporary, but what is unseen is eternal' (2 Cor. 4:18). Paul must have known that the urge to make ourselves comfortable in this world is very strong. He must have known that it's not only very strong, it's also, in the right measure, very good. In planting down in Dhulikhel, we were making deep connections with the people around us. We were wearing the same clothes, speaking the same language and very often crying and laughing over the same things. But even so, we were realising that in the scheme of things we were only temporary, we were like the grass that withers away, here today and gone tomorrow. Even if we didn't have to make use of our go-bag and leave in an emergency, we would still be leaving after a three-year period. So I began to realise that being temporary in that sense did make a difference to the way we lived. Although we were attaching ourselves to *people*, we weren't particularly attaching ourselves to *things* to the same degree as we had previously done in Australia. Knowing that we couldn't take our furniture and motorbike and swings back to Australia changed the way that we perceived them. We could enjoy them greatly but not rely on them. We could appreciate them without being gripped by them. And we could somehow even view hardships in the same way also. The trials of life in Dhulikhel challenged us to the core of our being but we knew that they, also, would pass – they were not eternal. A plane flight would bring them to a sudden and abrupt close.

As I sat there that afternoon I longed to somehow re-write the perspective on the colours of my soul. I wanted to learn to view my life on earth in the same way that I was learning to view my life in Dhulikhel. I wanted to enjoy and appreciate the beauty of it without being gripped by it. I wanted to plant deeply but keep my eyes fixed on heaven, knowing that the streets of gold would bring with them the restoration of all things.

6

THE KINGDOM OF GOD IS WITHIN YOU

The Dhulikhel Old Bazaar is aptly named. It's a maze of winding cobbled paths bordered by ancient brick buildings. Doors and windows are made of traditional woodcarvings. They sit so low that you have to almost bend double to enter them. Roofs are made of slate and straw and there is no glass to be seen anywhere. Our walk to Nepali church on Saturday mornings would take us straight through this architectural wonder. Small children would lean out of the carved wooden windows, 'Hello, *Namaste.*' Their eyes would light up as they made contact with us. 'What is your name? Hello!'

As we sent our greetings back, the sunlight would touch the tips of the Hindu shrines and the shutters in each shop would open to reveal strangely shaped cucumbers and chillies that lay in boxes by our feet. Tiny packets of hair shampoo dangled from strings and floated in the breeze. Then, we would reach the hospital corner and turn right. Two shops down the lane there was an old concrete building and in front of the entrance gate lay an overflowing gutter. We would slow down and give each other space to make the leap across it. None of us wanted to trip and end up in the mess below us. Past the gutter was the side door and then a dark corridor to reach the stairwell. The steps that took us to the third floor of the building were worn and chipped, so we took care as we climbed. Chickens darted out from under our feet, cackling their displeasure that their laying routine had been disturbed. Then the sound of Nepali choruses would waft down the stairs and we would hasten our steps, not wanting to miss a moment.

Outside the third-floor room there was a pile of discarded *chappals* and shoes as well as one or two motorbike helmets. We threw ours into the heap, quietly opened the door and made our way into church. The room was about the size of a large bedroom and empty of furniture. On the floor were some thin rugs, folded and making a patchwork effect on the bare concrete. The walls were also bare, black mould creeping around the windows and adding deepening shades to the whitewash. But within the room were twenty or so Nepalis, standing and singing their hearts out to God. Hands were raised high and faces were lifted, intent on worship. We crept in and joined them, pulling out our Nepali chorus book and finding the right page just in time for the song to finish. But the songs rolled on, one after another, reminding us in every breath of the One who reigns on this earth.

We turned with our friends to chorus number 23 and sang it very slowly, '*Prabhuma sadai anand garou, Pheri poni bandachu*' ('Rejoice in the Lord always and again I say rejoice'). We sang it over and over again. And as we sang, I looked around me. The two ladies in front of me had covered their heads with their worn scarves, the wool escaping from the spot where it had caught on burrs on the way to church. A little boy to the left of me was wearing a faded pink tracksuit that reached his shins and then petered out. His hands were lifted as he concentrated on worship. An older man to the right of me had his eyes closed, his gnarled hands clenched tightly together and his brow furrowed. I looked at him and wondered what he was thinking about as he sang.

And then I wondered – what was I thinking about as I sang? In what things do I rejoice? In what things do I put my trust?

Many of the extraneous things passed before my mind and I looked back at the people around me, who continued to lift their hands and sing. None of them owned a vehicle or a house. None of them owned a wardrobe full of clothes and none of them earned more than £5 a week. Yet, they lifted their faces and sang, 'Rejoice in the Lord always and again I say rejoice . . .' The more I sang with them, the more I lifted my face also.

In September of that year, twelve young people from the church were baptised. On the Saturday prior to the baptisms, our Nepali pastor invited them to share their testimonies with the people of the church. So, they lined up one by one, in the front of the room, nervous and halting, and took their turns to speak.

'My life is very hard,' said the first one in Nepali. 'I don't know where to turn to. My brother is missing, I failed my exams and we don't have enough food . . . But last year I prayed to Jesus and he gave me *shanti* (peace). Before, I used to bow down in front of gods of stone and I didn't feel peace. I felt *oshanti* (a lack of peace) all of the time. I felt fear and I worried about our country. But now, since I have prayed to Jesus, I have *shanti*. I have *shanti* all of the time; even though things are still bad, I have *shanti* inside.' He smiled at us and sat down while the next young man began to speak.

I sat and listened to all twelve of them and they all seemed to say the same thing. 'Before I had no peace but now I have God's peace – even in this time of war.'

Once a month after the regular church service in Dhulikhel, the women would stay to meet together and encourage one another. I remember the Saturday in November when it was Jalpa's turn to prepare the small devotion. She sat cross-legged and fiddled with the hem of her simple *lungi* (wraparound skirt that reaches to the ankles). She began by apologising, '*Moph garnos malai* . . . I'm so sorry.' She looked down at her lap

again and the shadows shifted on her face. 'I'm not well stud-
ied and I can't read very well. I don't know very much and I
can't speak very well . . .' Then, she slowly lifted her eyes to
meet the group, as if gathering courage. 'But this morning I
read from Luke chapter 6 and it spoke to me.'

She began to read haltingly from the Beatitudes in her
Nepali Bible:

> Blessed are you who are poor,
>   for yours is the kingdom of God.
> Blessed are you who hunger now,
>   for you will be satisfied.
> Blessed are you who weep now,
>   for you will laugh.
> Blessed are you when men hate you,
>   when they exclude you and insult you
>   and reject your name as evil,
>   because of the Son of Man.
> Rejoice in that day and leap for joy, because great is your
>   reward in heaven.
>
> (Luke 6:20–23)

Jalpa slowly finished the reading and once again met our eyes.
She told us, bravely, that she knew who she was. She knew
that she was poor. She knew that the small handful of rupees
that came into her home was not quite enough to feed everyone. Her husband only occasionally found work as a daily
labourer, and it was a struggle. She explained that she often
ran out of kerosene for the tiny burner that sat in the corner of
their single room. She didn't even have a hook for their
clothes.

But she also explained that she knew God. She said that
knowing God had changed her life. No – she wanted that clar-
ified. It had not changed her outer life. Not in the slightest. Her

outer struggles still continued, just as before. She was still hungry. She was still cold. But knowing God, had changed her inner life. She told us of the peace she now had within her. She told us about the peace that gave her strength every morning. She told us about the peace that gave her a hope for the future – a future with God. She told us that she was blessed, because hers was the kingdom of God. I looked at the smile on her face and her hands now folded neatly in her lap – and I believed her.

Two weeks later, Jalpa was diagnosed with an inoperable brain tumour. She was my age, 36. Her three children were the same ages as my three children. And it was winter. I went to visit her in the tiny room with the single bed and the kerosene burner in it. I opened the door and saw her huddled in a corner, wrapped up in her quilt while the breeze whistled through the newspaper in the window. Then I closed the door quietly behind me and tried not to cry. After we chatted and prayed, I checked her rice supplies in the corner and then walked slowly to the local shop in order to re-stock. My feet felt as heavy on the stony path as they have ever felt. We prayed and prayed. I gave her my warm woollen gloves. Others provided funds for radiotherapy and she rattled into the hospital at Banepa on the local bus to have the treatment.

She had the treatment, but she didn't appear to be improving. Very slowly, over the next month, Jalpa's face began to swell. And then her right eye closed up so that she could no longer see. On Christmas Day, she arrived at church but she held her *kasto* tightly over her head so that it covered that side of her face. She sang, but she sang very quietly, softer than a whisper. I moved into the space beside her and was aware of the effort as she tried to bring one of her legs out from under her. In front of us, the children were getting ready to put on a nativity play. Jalpa's middle daughter, Rahel, had wrapped a brown scarf around her head and was kneeling down on the bamboo mat, pretending to be a shepherd. Her son had borrowed his dad's *topi* and was pretending to be a wise man. I leaned further to my right, giving Jalpa more room to watch them with her left eye. And then we sang again, staying sitting on the floor. For Jalpa, it was too difficult to stand.

After church that day, I walked slowly home with Darren and the boys, through the Old Bazaar and past the doughnut man and the metalworker. We stopped to buy doughnuts and watched the man on the other side of the road as he formed gods out of copper and other bits of scrap metal. He poured the mixture into well-formed moulds and waited until they were set, ready to transform into gods. We ate our doughnuts and kept walking.

For the entire thirty-minute walk from the church to our home, there were no signs of Christmas – no tinsel, no lights, no trees and no presents. Instead, people were wrapping themselves in their *kastos* and making their way down to the bazaar to buy another three onions and a tomato or two. Others were lighting fires in the gutter and squatting beside them in an effort to keep warm. But inside my head were the words that Jalpa had shared with us six weeks earlier, 'Blessed are you who are poor, for yours is the kingdom of God. Blessed are you who hunger now, for you will be satisfied. Blessed are you who weep now, for you will laugh.' I looked around me at the absence of all the external signs of Christmas and felt abundantly blessed, because, like Jalpa and because of God's son, the kingdom of God was within me.

7

HE DRANK THE CUP

I will always remember that 1 February 2005 fell on a Tuesday. Tuesdays were our favourite day in Dhulikhel. After a morning of home-school we would eat our bread, straight from the machine, at twice the normal speed. We would then fight at the door over shoes and hats and burst through it, bubbling with the energy and anticipation required to make the journey over to the Howes's house.

Our Irish friends, who worked at the university teaching engineering and English, lived an hour's walk away – across the town, down the hill, through the paddy fields and up the other side of the hill past the pigs and the goats. Actually, initially, the journey took nearly two hours, but the cup of Irish tea and the cheerful faces at the end of it were worth it. They were more than worth it. They were the pivot of the week, the spark that kept us counting hours and checking the calendar – just in case Tuesday had crept around again unnoticed while we weren't looking.

This particular Tuesday had come in the normal, heavily anticipated way. We bubbled all the way down our hill and as far as the pipal tree. That was when we were met with the news. It seemed to spring out from nowhere, immediately taking centre stage.

'You shouldn't be out. King Gyanendra has just taken over the country. He's sacked the government and the prime minister.

He's cut all forms of communication within the country and . . .' our informant paused for breath, knowing he had our attention '. . . there's a nationwide full *bandh* as of 12 p.m.' He started to wave his hands and I looked down at my watch. It was 1 p.m.

'Quick!' he said again. 'You need to go back inside. It could be dangerous.'

Our anticipation fizzled out like a flame that had lost its oxygen supply. The skips that had carried us down the hill had no more reason to exist. Our feet somehow turned 180° and landed heavily, one after the other towards our house.

'But Mum! Why can't we go?' Jeremy tried to tug us back in the direction of the Irish tea.

'Well – you see the king has taken over the country and the people he's taken over from might get a little bit cross.'

We made it all the way back up our hill and through the maroon gate, our legs and voices protesting. The key still worked in our front door, which seemed vaguely surprising. I put down the bags in the hall and noticed that the inside of the house looked just the same as when we had left it half an hour ago. It was as if I expected the visuals of life to look different without a government.

I walked into the living room, still looking for the differences and needing a concrete indicator that I wasn't dreaming. I found it within arm's reach. The phone was dead. I sat down and held it to my ear for a long time, listening to the silence that accompanies a vacuum – a vacuum that was designed for noise. I sat there listening and tried to imagine a whole country without a single phone operating, landline or mobile. I tried to imagine a whole country without email and without any contact with the outside world. I tried to imagine a whole country now relying on heavily censored newspapers and a radio station controlled by the king. It felt like the plane had gone off the radar screen and Nepal was, for the first time, an island.

Darren was supervising a clinical placement at a hospital in Kathmandu that week. He probably wouldn't be able to get home.

When would we see him again? How long would it go on? Exactly a month prior to this we'd had an email from the INF security team. They had heard that the king might do such a thing and were hypothesising that there could be a massive reaction to this from the political parties, in the form of violent outbursts. So the warning was that we could find ourselves in an extended period of hibernation. We needed to have at least enough dry goods and food in the pantry to last a month.

A month. Hmmm – I left the phone and walked back into the kitchen. Piled onto the cane shelf in front of me were a few tuna tins, three onions, one packet of pasta, three packets of biscuits, fifteen eggs, peanut butter, half a container of rice and the same again of flour. We prayed. The kids had afternoon tea and I started to count the biscuits. If we had thirty-two altogether and there were five of us, how many days would that last us?

While I was redoing my times tables, Darren arrived home on his bicycle. Apparently bicycles can get through even the worst of *bandhs*. He took off his helmet and we hugged him more than we normally did. Chris and Jeremy wrapped themselves like koalas around his legs. We even let him have three biscuits.

It seemed that things were very uncertain in Kathmandu. That night and the next morning we kept tuning in to Nepal news and checking the local paper. We heard that the airport was closed and international flights diverted. We heard that as well as sacking the coalition government led by Sher Bahadur Deuba, the king had also declared a state of emergency. That meant that certain rights were no longer available to citizens: freedom of opinion, freedom of speech, freedom of the press, freedom of communication, freedom of movement, freedom of privacy, freedom of property, freedom to assemble in groups.

> Considering the nation and national interest, His Majesty's Government has banned for six months any interview, article, news, notice, view or personal opinion that goes against the letter and spirit of the Royal Proclamation on 1 Feb 2005. Action will be taken against anyone violating this notice. (*Kathmandu Post*)

Reading the *Kathmandu Post* soon called for even more imagination than it normally did. The morning after the announcement, the paper arrived at our breakfast table in the ordinary way. We glanced at it over the porridge bowl and saw that instead of the normal gruesome images, the front page now showed a beautiful picture of a lake with geese swimming across it. Inside the paper, the articles of information had also transformed. Instead of the usual accounts of violence and torture, there were now long quotes from King Gyanendra justifying his actions and promising the restoration of multiparty democracy within three years. He said that the political parties had not been dealing effectively with the Maoist problem. Instead, they had been using their resources to jostle for power and that wasn't in the nation's best interests. Hence the royal takeover and the arrest of 43 political leaders and student activists by the palace army. Around each of the quotes there were pictures of people hailing King Gyanendra and carrying large portraits of him and his wife, Queen Komal.

In Dhulikhel, our phone remained dead for all of February. It seemed to us to be quite a long time to be without any means of communication. INF's headquarters in those years was in Pokhara, 240 kilometres away, so that meant that we had no idea what INF's overall plan was, if they had one . . . We felt cut off. To deal with these feelings, we regularly walked down to the bazaar and sat and listened to the conversations in Nepali that flowed all around us. We tuned in to the opinions of our Nepali neighbours and waited for something tangible within the vacuum. Initially, most of the opinions seemed positive.

'Perhaps King Gyanendra can do something, he's right, the political parties were hopeless; give him a go, wait and see, things were terrible the way they were.'

We waited to hear as many opinions as we could and then we walked back home and checked the phone – and it was silent.

One of the phone calls that we wanted to make during that time, was to Darren's mother, Jan, who was due to fly out and visit us in the coming weeks. We worried that if we couldn't contact her in time, she might cancel her flights and that would be awful. Visitors from Australia were a bit like Tuesday afternoons, only better. Not only did they come stocked up with goodies and news and gifts, they also brought with them a fresh perspective of the land we lived in – and a fresh inspiration to serve. So, one night during the first week of February, while we were worrying about Jan and her flights, we went next door to pray with John and Margaret. As well as the phone being dead, the *bijuli* (electricity) was also off, so we sat in the dim light and went around the circle, sharing our concerns.

Margaret listened to our worries and then leaned forward in her chair, pleading with God. 'Oh Lord, please let the phones come back on – even if they came back on just for half an hour, that would be wonderful.'

I felt myself smile as I listened to her prayer and then we returned home. I went into the living area to pick up the phone, more as a joke than anything. But as I listened, my eyes widened – the dialling tone had come back on! I put the phone back down and it rang instantly. I picked it up again and immediately heard the rise and fall of Jan's excited greeting.

Her sing-song voice echoed around the lounge as we confirmed her flights and reassured her that we were all perfectly well. We were anticipating her arrival, state of emergency or not. She sounded, understandably, relieved. Then I placed the receiver back down and once again checked the dial tone. It had disappeared.

The phone lines were cut off for another three weeks in Dhulikhel without even thirty minutes of relief. We later found out that during those thirty minutes that we had a phone line, it had been midnight in Sydney. Jan had felt prompted to call us, and she'd acted on the prompt. If only I could do that more often . . .

On 8 February, seven days after the royal takeover, Darren again left for work in Kathmandu. He needed to stay there overnight for a physio meeting. So the boys and I trooped upstairs to start home-school at 8 a.m., knowing that we were looking down the barrel of a longish day. It's always long if Daddy isn't coming home. Nevertheless, we would attack it in the usual way.

We were doing fine. Then at 9.30 a.m. everything began to move. I was walking through the school room door and I watched as the cupboard across the hall seemed to move backwards and forwards. Stephen's desk shuddered and all his pens slipped across and onto the floor. I could hear the chink of the glasses downstairs as they shifted towards each other in the cabinet. My eyes moved back to the cupboard which seemed to have settled in one place again. Chris and Jeremy were having an extended morning tea in their bedroom. Stephen slipped out from behind his desk and met me under the doorframe. He knows what to do in an earthquake, but his eyes held the question. Do we need to go outside? Should we run? What if there's more?

I called for Chris and Jeremy and we all tumbled down the stairs and headed outside, just in case. We stood still and quiet in the front courtyard as I tried to imagine which way the walls would move, if it were to happen again. Then I checked for electricity wires above us and thought about the pine trees on the other side of the courtyard. We waited for quite some time but, fortunately, there was no second act. Earthquakes were and still are one of my biggest fears. Most experts agree that Kathmandu is long overdue for a big one, which has in no way added to my sense of safety.

After some time, we braved going back into the house and I headed to the kitchen to fill up the kettle and pop it on the gas burner. But I turned the tap all the way around to the left and nothing came out. Nothing at all. I stared at the emptiness beneath the tap and tried to make sense of it. Our water supply was hardly ever cut off in Dhulikhel. So of course I thought, what if the epicentre of the earthquake was in Kathmandu? How would I know? I had no phone or means of contacting anyone. And again, what about Darren? Where's he?

Then, immediately after the water vanished, and right behind me in the kitchen, Jeremy started throwing up. It was not a good combination. I had no husband, no phone, no water, an earthquake, a royal takeover, a state of emergency and a child throwing up. I looked around me and wondered how to clean up the mess without any water. I grabbed the nearest rag and started to wipe Jeremy's face. Chris started heaving and moaning about the smell. I tried to manoeuvre them all out of the way and back upstairs to the school room. And as I did so, my feet dragged on the stairs and I became aware of a sense of dread.

It might also have been the newspaper article that I had read that morning at breakfast: 'Despite peace overtures made this week to the Maoists, the army's spokesman warned of a long and bloody battle before the Maoists are weak enough to be forced to the negotiating table . . .' My feet took the stairs one at a time and at the same time as worrying about Jeremy, the water and the earthquake I thought about the 15,000 hard-core Maoist fighters as well as their 50,000 militiamen. Then I thought of the villagers and the low-caste tribes who, having nothing to gain from the political status quo, had looked to the Maoists as their only hope for a better life. And I felt dread within me.

But it was more than just the dread of what might erupt politically. It was the dread of what might erupt again under the earth, underneath our boys. For that entire day and night this feeling of dread overwhelmed me. It sat like a bag of weights on my spine. I staggered under the weight of it. My lungs took in less air as I anticipated the awful possibilities. I somehow managed to put the boys to bed. I checked their closed eyes and measured breathing once again before I made my way back downstairs. The house was terribly still. And as I entered the kitchen I prayed, 'Lord, do you understand this feeling of dread? I mean, you understand all things. You have experienced all things. But do you *really*? Do you really know about *dread*?'

The water had come back on so I started the washing up. There's nothing quite like washing up in times of trial. It's almost as good as hanging out the clothes. I was halfway through the cups and still aware of the terrible weight that clung to me. I knew that I was not doing well. So I thought to myself, 'What I need is chocolate, or music, or anything comforting . . .' I left the washing up and rummaged in the bottom of the pantry and found an old bar of Indian chocolate and then I put my favourite CD on. The fifth song on the CD was 'Consider Christ'.

The song came to an end and the house was so quiet I could hear the walls thinking. The washing up was forgotten. He knows dread – of course he knows dread. As the lyrics reminded me, though Jesus was full of dread and fearful of what he was about to face, he still drank the cup that was reserved for me. And in that moment of silence in my kitchen it became much less about 'does he understand me?' and much more about me coming a tiny bit closer to understanding what he'd done for me. The image of Gethsemane was very real for me that night. The house seemed to echo with the pain and the suffering, the fear and the anguish. I re-understood dread. As my Lord waited in the garden that night, he was *full* of dread, the dread of a certain future. He was not dreading an uncertain future, a possible earthquake or a bloody battle – he was dreading an inescapable agonising death, a cold-blooded murder.

That night in my kitchen I saw his bent body, twisting and falling onto his face, weighed down with anguish. I saw him shaking and the sweat turning to blood and pouring off him as he cried out. I heard his voice become hoarse and then fall to a whisper, 'Father, take it away. Please take it away. It's possible for you. All things are possible for you . . . But yet, not my will. Yours.'

And so, that night as I realised that Jesus was full of dread, I also realised that he could see beyond it. He endured the cross, the suffering and the shame because of the 'joy set before him' (Hebrews 12:2). He endured it because of us. He endured it because of me. He endured it so that I could share in the joy set before him.

And I went to bed – and slept.

8

BEING CONTENT

By March, the phone lines had been restored in Dhulikhel and Jan had also arrived safe and sound with her bags of goodies and stories of life back in Australia. She settled in quickly and was soon running preschool with Jeremy so that I could concentrate my energies on Stephen and Chris – who had by then started kindergarten. At the same time, the United States and India had begun to put pressure on the king, calling on him to restore the democratic process. They asked for a return of civil liberties and freedom of the media as well as the release of those under house arrest. The king responded by saying that the state of emergency would be a short-term measure only. But he didn't say how long it would be.

In response, the Maoists announced another indefinite blockade of the major roads coming in and out of Kathmandu. And in response to that, the palace army launched a massive operation to keep the roads open. In the midst of all this, an old man who lived in the southern flat plains of Nepal somehow made his way up to Kathmandu and then to Dhulikhel and arrived at our church one Saturday morning. His bent figure moved slowly and carefully as he walked to the front of the church. He negotiated the crossed legs, the sari folds and the Bibles laid out on the floor. A child reached up to touch him and his hand reached down to meet hers. Then he turned slowly to face us. We saw his lined face and we waited for his words.

'You know in Nepal it's *always* been good to meet together in fellowship, in churches and in home groups.' He paused and looked thoughtful. 'But in these days, in these days of civil war and strife, it's *even better.*'

He smiled as he spoke to us and I thought about his words, as well as his life. Here was an old man who had seen his country move from peace to war in the final decade of his life. He'd seen his own people rise up against each other in unmitigated violence. He must have looked about him and felt the sadness of it, like a lump that just sits there and can never be swallowed. He must have grieved for his nation and his people. Yet in his lifetime, he'd also seen the birth of the church. He'd seen it grow from a handful of believers in 1952 to 700,000 people across the country professing faith in Jesus in 2005. In fifty years he'd seen all of this and more. He'd been part of the growth and he wanted to share it with us. But mostly he wanted to share with us the link that exists between growth and hardship. That's because he knew that there was a link. 'In these days of civil war, fellowship is even better.'

I listened to his words and I asked myself the questions, 'What exactly is it that makes fellowship *even better* during civil war? What is it that makes church services more memorable? What is it that makes faithful dependence more remarkable?' He continued with his testimony and I slowly felt stirred to agree with him. My mind didn't grasp all his words, even less his experiences, yet I acknowledged the truth he painted that morning. I acknowledged it while knowing that I was unable to articulate it for myself. I merely wrote it down.

The following week, we once again headed over to Pokhara for our annual INF conference. But this time we didn't sit for ten hours on a bus. We flew. Road travel was deemed too risky with the unresolved tensions between the Maoists and the army. The Himalayas rose steadily to our right for the thirty-minute flight and then we made our way up the Pokhara valley to the INF compound. We settled ourselves down onto the plastic seats beneath the folds of our conference tent along with sixty others, who had also struggled through the uncertainties of the previous month. Some of them had arrived by helicopter, having no other means of transport out of their more remote centres. In front of us, our INF Director welcomed us to the conference and we began to sing.

And it was relief. It was *even better*. Perhaps the longer the journey is or the more uncertain its outcome, the more I long for fellowship, the more I value it, the more I need it. That week at the INF conference, while political strife carried on outside the tent, inside the tent fellowship had never seemed richer.

After the conference, we returned home to Dhulikhel and Jan returned home to Australia. It was the first week in April and I realised that it was a whole year since I had taught the physio students. By then, Darren had given up on trying to transform the calendar with red pen but I surprised him by actually offering to do some more teaching. And he accepted. So I made my way out of the front door that week, much less loaded down by text books, and he stayed home to school the boys. And it all worked out really well. Darren even admitted that home-school had been so relaxing that he'd actually fallen asleep during story-writing. The weather had become quite balmy which probably added to the siesta-like feeling. Outside in our garden the plum trees were blossoming again and tiny green plums were starting to appear. In the terraces, the corn had been replaced by early bean shoots and Srijana had been busy harvesting the garlic.

It was balmy and relaxing in our garden but, to be honest, the build-up of tension outside our gate was beginning to wear me down. We had been in Nepal for eighteen months and I was feeling tired. I could tell that I was tired by my responses to the world beyond the gate. The sights and sounds

of the bazaar no longer drew my attention. The dirt was familiar, as was the line of washing-up water which trailed across
the path and joined the other plastic rubbish in the gutter. The
sounds of the early morning bells that called the Hindus to
worship were beginning to ring in annoying waves within my
head.

And it was about then that I realised that it's the *living* of
truth that's the hard bit. I can pack truth into my mind and
memorise scripture, but I struggle with the living – especially
the living when no one else is watching. Even when they are
watching, I struggle within my head: I complain, I feel resent-
ful, I long for something easier. It's a constant theme of mine
but it can begin during any unremarkable moment.

That month in Dhulikhel it began at the local shop. I was sitting there on the little cane stool, once again staring into the
dim recesses of the open shelving that lined each of the three
walls. I was letting my eyes hover on the packets of coconut
biscuits that sat next to the peanuts and then slowly moved
around to the cakes of soap and the jars of Horlicks. Next to
the Horlicks were the tins of tuna and the oil, the spices, the
teabags and finally the locally made porridge. Below the
shelving were the sacks of rice and lentils and flour and sugar.
Above the shelving were the uncalled-for items like the toilet
paper. And hanging in strings from the ceiling were the tiny
packets of shampoo and the red betel nut. My eyes lingered on
each item, seeing them and not seeing them, hoping for more
and seeing less; longing for a new idea that would transform
the meals that were coming out of our kitchen.

I didn't find it. Instead, I saw in my mind, the aisles of our
supermarket near our home in the Blue Mountains. I saw
myself with my trolley laden down with muesli bars and
Weet-Bix and approaching the dairy aisle. I saw a whole aisle
of yoghurt and cheese. I could almost feel the drips of mois-
ture that rested on the yoghurt containers and I could almost

hear the groan of the trolley wheels as I added to my supply. It was almost too much to bear. There was no cheese or yoghurt or Weet-Bix or muesli bars to be found in Dhulikhel. I opened my eyes and smiled at the *sahuji*. I slowly asked for 2 kilograms of yellow lentils and she began to scoop them out of the sack and weigh them. Then with her back to me, she began to speak.

'Tomorrow there is a festival in Dhulikhel. A god is coming.'

'Oh really?' I said. I watched as the horizontal beam of the hanging scales came to rest in a place of equilibrium. 'When is he coming?'

'Actually, he's already come.' She began to pour the lentils into a piece of newspaper and wrap them into a ball. 'He came yesterday.'

I reached for the lentils and placed them in my bag next to the sack of rice.

'Who is he, this god?' I waited till she looked up. 'What's his name and why does he come?'

'Well . . .' she paused, 'I'm not sure of his name or why he comes. The problem is we have too many gods. We're not like you, we have too many to count and we have too many to name.' She scribbled down the price of lentils and rice on a piece of paper and counted out my change, and as she did so, we kept chatting.

We spoke for quite a while. And as we spoke, I heard God whisper to me, 'Where would you rather be? In the supermarket in Australia with the Weet-Bix and the cheese and the full trolley or here with the lentils and this lady who wants to talk to you?'

'Here, Lord,' I said very softly, before I said goodbye, picked up my bag and walked home.

But discontent didn't just seep out in the local shop. After a year of home-school, we were still enjoying the opportunities and the freedom, but for me, the days were beginning to drag.

There were so many mornings that went wrong. The one I remember most clearly was the one when Jeremy dropped the glass Horlicks jar and Chris spilt the milk *and* Stephen moaned about doing his jobs. I looked at my watch and realised that we were due to start school in three minutes' time. I also noticed that the electricity had gone off which meant that I couldn't start the washing machine or put the bread on for lunch. While I was wondering what we could eat for lunch, Jeremy began shouting for help. He couldn't finish the rest of his porridge because there was no more Horlicks. His hands were waving at the floor which was covered in brown powder and slivers of shattered glass.

I stared at the light as it reflected off the bits of glass and knew that that particular morning I had reached the end of me. I had nothing left to give that day, the next day, or any day. In a daze, I cleaned up the kitchen and we went upstairs and found our way through maths and English and science. By 3 p.m. I was sitting alone on the back porch, staring out at the clouds that hovered around the mountains and desiring patience more than I had ever desired anything.

But as I fixed my eyes on the horizon, I was aware of only one thought: 'You can desire it. You can ask for it. You can break down and cry out loud. But that's not how you get patience. The only way to grow in patience is to walk a path where patience is required. It comes when it's practised.' There were no easy answers. There were no easy solutions. I breathed in deeply and returned to the stage where I would learn it.

One day, I was bemoaning my situation. I was feeling so limited in the things that I could do and the people I could see. Even when I did have a free moment, it was difficult to make the most of it. Although we had a phone that occasionally worked, most of my Nepali friends didn't. I couldn't ring anyone or invite them over. So I sat there and longed for a time and a place where I could once again walk out of the door when I wanted to and make deliberate attempts at relationships, either through work or play. I longed for a place that was somewhere else. I thought, reasonably, that the grass 'somewhere else' would be greener. I remember closing my eyes and longing for it. And as I longed for it, the grass in the other place seemed so close that I could almost feel the imprint that it might leave on the soles of my feet.

And of course that afternoon a Nepali woman in great need arrived at my door. As I invited her in, I caught again a whiff of something new. I couldn't go out and make relationships but that didn't stop them from coming to the door. That evening in Dhulikhel, after closing the door behind the woman, I smiled at myself and the question came again, 'Where would you rather be?'

'Here, Lord,' I said again, very softly.

The same question, the same response, but that year I seemed to need to learn it over and over again. I even learnt it while teaching Sunday school in our Dhulikhel church. Each week the twenty children would pack into a room which was only just bigger than our kitchen. The room was actually the pastor's daughters' bedroom, so it held two small wooden beds and a cupboard as well as the twenty children sitting cross-legged on the bamboo mats covering the lino floor. The first morning that I taught them, I smiled and greeted them in Nepali. I told them who I was, just in case they hadn't guessed. Then I asked if someone would like to pray.

Someone did. Jalpa's daughter Rahel stuck her hand straight up, then proceeded to pray in Nepali for me, for the group, for our boys, for the church, for her mother, for the pastor, for the nation, for everything she could think of – in a voice that must have made the angels smile. It made me smile. I'd never heard a child pray like that before. She went on for so long that I even peeked out at her during the prayer to check that everything was alright. I saw her hands still clasped tightly together, her eyes squeezed shut, her head bowed and her dark plaits hanging together. I quickly closed my eyes again and prayed for the gift of concentration in worship.

The children taught it to me. For the next two hours, we all sat there on the floor, reading the Bible, singing, praying and singing some more. It felt as though the bamboo mat had made permanent patterns on my backside before it was time to stand up again. I noticed, though, that the children weren't complaining. They were still singing. Over the next few months, I tried to introduce craft and drama, colouring and dialogue, puzzles and role-play. They showed great appreciation, but it was still singing that they really wanted to do. As we rolled into the second hour each Saturday, I would find myself wondering how worship compared with the rest of their week: manual labour, water collecting, the struggle to survive. Of course they wanted to be at church. Of course they wanted to sing. Wouldn't we all? But somehow, the desire to be in church, the desire for worship had seeped into a deeper level of their beings, until it oozed out at the pores.

Then, one Friday night during April I was terribly tired and I was sitting tucked up in bed trying to translate the rest of the Sunday school lesson for the following morning. My eyes stared at the *dev nagari* script (the script in which Nepali is written) and the conjugated verb that I was searching for simply didn't come. My mind was as empty as the page. So I closed my eyes, and as I did so a thought came. Wouldn't it be so much easier if I could be somewhere else, if I could teach Sunday school in English. It would be so much quicker! Just think of the hours I would save in translations. I could even speak off the top of my head. I could tell stories and talk normally. The grass would be so much greener.

Somehow I opened my eyes, finished the lesson, bordered on resentment and then succumbed to sleep. In the morning, I was still aware of the thoughts. I was aware of them as we walked through the bazaar and patted the goats. I was aware of them as I removed my *chappals* and walked into the Sunday school. I was aware of them as I sat down. And then the children began to sing – and the thoughts left. The grass was greener where I sat.

It went on like that for almost all of 2005. I was oscillating. One minute I would be growing in contentment and learning to appreciate the time and the place that God had me. But the next minute, out of the blue, I would be once again longing for somewhere else, somewhere easier or more comfortable. If nothing else, it was exhausting. And then I would sit on our back porch and read the passage from Paul's letter to the Philippians and I would wonder how on earth he did it:

> I have learned to be content whatever the circumstances. I know what it is to be in need, and I know what it is to have plenty. I have learned the secret of being content in any and every situation, whether well fed or hungry, whether living in plenty or in want. I can do everything through him who gives me strength. (Phil. 4:11–13)

Paul says that he has 'learned to be content'. No matter how many times I read over that passage in Dhulikhel, it still came out as past tense. He's not learning it, he has *learned* it. As I sat on our back porch, I wondered how he could say that. I wondered even more so how he'd learned it. Did he have a secret?

While I was wondering we became friends with a family who were originally from Sri Lanka. They had come to Kathmandu University to teach biological sciences and they had two small children with them.

Although we knew about their arrival plans, we'd been told that the university was sorting out their accommodation. So on their second day in Dhulikhel we invited them and John

and Margaret and the Howes family over for a meal and to
pray. They all knocked at the door and we invited them in,
introducing everyone and sorting out hats and shoes and bags
in the flurry at the front door. At the same time, the boys led
all the children out into the back garden, showing them the
pets and the forts and the hideouts. They caught on quickly
and began to add to their pile of home-made bows and
arrows. It was all going very well.

Then, as we sat down to pray, Sam and Deshi told us that
there had been some kind of mix-up in their accommodation
which meant that they were without a home by their second
night in Dhulikhel. We looked at their faces and didn't know
what to say. We tried to imagine that it was us – the long journey from another country, the fatigue, the piles of luggage, the
inability to speak in the language of the people, the stress of
not knowing what was going on – and then finding out that
their accommodation had not been sorted out.

While we stared at them in horror, somebody suggested that
we pray and so we did – quite fervently – surely God had a
solution in mind. So we went around the circle and took it in
turns to pray – and managed to come up with a whole variety
of our own solutions. But it was only after we all paused for
breath that Sam prayed. And I will never forget the words that
he used. It was more what he didn't pray. He didn't pray for a
place to stay or for any kind of resolution to their problem. He
didn't even mention the fact that the family were without
beds. Instead, he prayed this, in the quietest voice I've ever
heard: 'Lord, when I'm most distressed, help me to bring glory
to you.'

That was all. In the silence that followed, I kept my eyes
closed and a single thought came. I want to be able to pray like
that. I want to be able to keep my eyes on him like that.

Some weeks later, the Sri Lankan family had sorted out their
accommodation and they introduced us to an Indian family

whom they'd met at the university. Because this family were only going to be in Nepal for twelve months they hadn't brought many of their worldly goods with them. Gradually, we came to know them and to share meals with them as well as with the wider group. If the meal was at our house, we would borrow plates from John and Margaret and we would have just enough cutlery for everyone. But if the meal was at their house, we would take it in turns to eat, each using and then passing on the four plastic forks and four dishes that they owned. Then, after the rice and curry, came the best bit. Muriel turned out to be a fantastic custard maker and she had begun to save all her old tuna tins. After a good wash and the removal of the plastic wrappers, the tuna tins made a perfectly sized dessert bowl. She would pour in little blobs of custard and mix it with banana and we would once again share plastic spoons and retrieve the custard from the corners of the tuna tin. It was delicious.

But we not only shared the forks and the tuna tins, over time we shared gratitude. It seemed that every time Muriel opened her mouth it was a testimony to the way that God was at work in her life – and it was done in such a gentle way that it also drew us into his presence and his comfort. And the more that we shared in her stories and in his comfort, the more the plastic spoons became irrelevant. Over time, all that came to matter was being able to meet together to pray, to encourage one another and to look to God in the concerns before us. And because the fellowship was so rich, the custard in the tuna tins also became rich – it even felt like the height of indulgence to be sitting there, two on each plastic seat, eating Muriel's custard out of a tuna tin. I would scrape the last blob from my little tin and watch the faces of my new friends as they also placed their tins on the table. It was a picture of contentment and, somehow, it opened up the picture that Paul was describing in Philippians.

And then the more I thought about it during those months, the more I realised that growing in contentment was much the same as growing in patience. Perhaps the only way to grow in contentment was to walk a path where contentment was required. Paul had done that. He had been well-fed and hungry. He had known plenty and want. He had known shipwrecks and jail terms and beatings and danger. He had realised that we not only suffer from lack of contentment when we face deprivation but also and equally so, when we face prosperity. And perhaps the question of contentment was related to my earlier questions about being able to see the unseen. In longing for something easier or a place or a situation where the grass seemed greener, I was always and automatically longing for Australia. I was picturing it, in all its splendour. And so often, that's what I do. When I'm discontent, I let my eyes linger on the place or the people or the things that would solve the problem. But maybe I needed to once again replace the images of Australia with the streets of gold – heaven – the only place where the grass really is greener.

Paul did know the secret. He knew how to keep his eyes on heaven and he knew that he found contentment in one place only – in him, the Lord God, who gives him, and us, the strength that we need for the situation we find ourselves in.

9

THE UNSEEN

Nepalis are used to rain. The fact that it rains for 110 days in a row from the first week in June to the last week in September is not really remarkable to them. Rain means rice harvest and rice harvest means food. One day in June 2005 our neighbour Margaret was teaching English at the local Nepali school. The beating of the rain on the old tin roof was so loud that she couldn't even hear her own words. A small girl at the side of the room raised her hand with a query and Margaret had to move closer to hear the words. 'Excuse me, Miss, but the rain is dripping on my desk.'

Margaret had not been in Nepal for five years for nothing. She took it in her stride. 'Oh well, dear, just move your desk forward a bit until you're out of the rain.'

Nepalis might be used to 110 days of consecutive rain but I, even after living through seven monsoons, am not. I start to feel hemmed in as soon as the calendar moves to June. The official date for Nepal's monsoon arrival is usually around the 10 June. Every now and again there is a delay by a day or two if the jet stream is late in leaving the Himalayas, but generally the monsoon arrives perfectly on time. Indeed, if it didn't, there would be widespread famine across the Asian sub-continent because the rice would not be able to be planted out.

The monsoon of 2005 started in the ordinary way. It was delayed by two days but then a low-pressure system turned the bay arm of the monsoon into a sharp north-westerly direction and the four-month torrent began. The mountains were covered by thick black cloud and the fog sat heavily in the valley before us. Even the mud houses that normally sat precariously on our nearby ridge were blackened into oblivion. I watched from the back porch as the rain poured down in streams from the roof of our house. It splashed into the mud beneath the swings and made a thudding noise on the roof of the chicken coop. It splattered off the banana leaves and landed in showers on the beans below them.

As I stood there and listened to its ceaseless teeming, I faced the grim reality of four months inside the house. Even in our home-school topics, the novelty of rain was wearing off. We'd already used up all our monsoon school topics the year before. We'd already identified the strange monsoonal insects and we'd already collected and then measured and re-measured litres of rain water. As I stood there in June and watched the rain soak into our garden, I faced the fact that I was already tired of it.

But by the end of June, it wasn't just the rain that was adding to my weariness. It was the contrast of it all. That year, after a difficult April, the month of May had been busy, full of exciting outings and visitors from Australia, as well as an ease in the political tensions. The month of May had begun by King Gyanendra lifting the three-month state of emergency. Although there were new orders banning political activities in major locations of Kathmandu and restricting media coverage, it still felt like a relief after three months of uncertainty. Then, also in May, my mum and her partner Keith arrived and became involved in the adventure of our lives in Dhulikhel. Through their fascination and questions, they added sparkle to what had become increasingly normal for us. Suddenly we also wanted to know how Nepalis dried their rice paper and what was the name of the huge orchid flowering on our hill.

In May, we had once again dived into life and tried to find out the answers to their questions. But then, at the end of the month, they stepped onto an aeroplane and flew into the sky while we stayed in Nepal, feeling the weight of their absence and the abruptness of their departure.

Then and almost worse, the Howes, our Irish friends who lived across the paddy fields, made the decision to relocate from Dhulikhel into Kathmandu. Their children were getting older and requiring secondary education. As we listened to their decision over more Irish tea and looked through the windows at all our children playing in the paddy fields, we nodded and agreed with them. We knew that it was a good and right decision for them. We would even have done the same thing, if it had been us. So we kept watching and nodding, even while feeling the loss within us. Without Tuesdays to look forward to, we weren't sure that we would be able to get through the weeks. And then, if the weeks became months of rain and if there were never any Tuesdays or never any reason to gobble down our fresh bread and race out of the door, how would we make it through them?

We weren't sure. And while we were wondering, the rain kept teeming down around us and hemming us in to our house. It was as if our lives were becoming slowly reduced to the life that took place inside our four walls. And that was not that exciting.

But while we were being hemmed in by the rain and the curfew, which was still being enforced at night, on the other side of Dhulikhel Jalpa lay in her tiny room, hemmed in by her body which was growing weaker and weaker. She was no longer able to stand or leave the room. Her husband began to stay at home and care for her and, as a result, their food supplies and meagre resources dwindled. One afternoon Darren came home from work early, so I braved the rain to go and visit her. I left my dripping umbrella and soaked *chappals* by the door and knocked quietly. There was no sound from within, so I gently eased open the door and crept in. She was alone in the room, her face shrunken and resting on the pillow. I moved towards her and sat down carefully on the bed. She didn't lift her head but her dry lips moved into a smile.

As we talked, I tried not to look about me at the room. I tried not to look at the bare whitewashed walls and the mould that had worsened with the monsoon. I tried not to notice the cracked lino or the smell of the pigs from next door that was drifting in through the window. I tried not to think of palliative care units back in Australia; of flowers and gentle music and beautiful pictures. I just watched her eyes and heard her voice as she talked about her hopes for heaven and her hopes for her family who she would leave behind. It seemed, as she talked, that Jalpa was seeing the unseen – as clearly as she ever had. And it seemed as if the mould on the walls around her was becoming less noticeable; it was already fading into a life that was temporary – here today and gone tomorrow. Later, Rahel came home from school and together we ran through the rain and across to the shops where we stocked up on food. Then we sloshed back down the hill with a sack of rice and tea and peanuts, our feet making squelching noises in the mud. We opened the door quietly, put the food down and I turned to say goodbye, but Jalpa had already fallen asleep.

Two weeks later, early on a Wednesday morning, the shrill tone of our phone echoed up the stairs and I tumbled out of bed to answer it. I raced down the stairs and picked it up, still rubbing my eyes while I listened to the greetings from our pastor. Then I listened to him as he told me slowly that Jalpa had died during the night. She'd struggled to breathe that evening and they had somehow taken her to the hospital, where she had died. I asked a few questions and then put the phone down heavily. I closed my eyes and saw in my mind her face, now with her eyes closed, too tired to lift them again.

The boys outside our house
in Dhulikhel

The view from our
bedroom window

Bagmati

Walking home from the bazaar

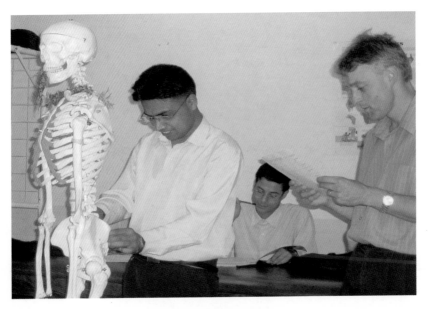

**Darren teaching at
DMI**

Visiting Srijana

Dhulikhel Church

A Nepali bus

Jalpa's funeral

Dal bhat on our
hill

**Physio graduation party at
our house**

**The army camp at the
bottom of the hill**

A roadblock

**On the way to
Mount Everest**

Kathmandu under daytime
curfew

Our farewell at Dhulikhel
Church

Because she was a Christian her body was not allowed to be kept on the hospital grounds. It was not allowed to be kept in any building overnight. Having no other options, the funeral was held the same day. Darren joined our pastor and the other men and travelled to the new grave site. They took a local bus ride and then walked for four kilometres to an isolated place by the river, bordered by overgrown nettles. They took three hours to dig the grave by hand, as the sweat poured down from their faces. Then they sang and prayed and lowered the wooden casket into the ground. They said goodbye to Jalpa . . . on a muggy July afternoon.

The following weekend we were back in church. The mood was quiet and reflective. Everybody was terribly sad. Everybody hurt for her husband and three small children. The songs were also much quieter than normal. We moved on to number 138, '*Chaddai aunnechon Yesu Raja*' ('Come Back Quickly, Lord Jesus'). There was a whispered longing as the tears began to form behind my eyes, 'Oh Lord, come quickly.'

Then, the pastor moved to the front and began to speak and he spoke from two different passages. The first was Luke 6:20–23:

> Blessed are you who are poor, for yours is the kingdom of God. Blessed are you who hunger now, for you will be satisfied. Blessed are you who weep now, for you will laugh. Blessed are you when men hate you, when they exclude you and insult you and reject your name as evil, because of the Son of Man. Rejoice in that day and leap for joy, because great is your reward in heaven.

I raised my head and listened to the ebb and flow of his voice. He didn't know that Jalpa had shared from that passage at the women's meeting seven months earlier. He didn't know that she had told us that she was blessed. He didn't know that she had told us about the peace within her, her hope for the future and her future with God. She had told us all of this, not knowing then how close it was. As I listened to the sounds of his voice, I felt some peace also. Jalpa would have agreed with him. Then, he moved on to his second passage, 2 Corinthians 4:13–18:

> It is written: 'I believed; therefore I have spoken.' With that same spirit of faith we also believe and therefore speak, because we know that the one who raised the Lord Jesus from the dead will also raise us with Jesus and present us with you in his presence . . . Therefore we do not lose heart. Though outwardly we are wasting away, yet inwardly we are being renewed day by day. For our light and momentary troubles are achieving for us an eternal glory that far outweighs them all. So we fix our eyes not on what is seen, but on what is unseen. For what is seen is temporary, but what is unseen is eternal.

And he talked very gently to us about the things that we know. We know that the one who raised the Lord Jesus from the dead will also raise us with Jesus and present us in his presence. We know that. We rely on it. We cling to it. And it's only because of *that* knowledge that we can fix our eyes on the unseen. It's only because of that knowledge that we don't lose heart. It's only because of that knowledge that we are being renewed day by day.

Later, as I walked home, I thought about my light and momentary troubles that I had moaned about only weeks earlier. I thought about the rain and the curfews and the intensity of home-school. I thought about the bread machine that was beginning to leak and the cupboards that were mouldy again. And I realised once again that the demands of the visible monsoon were blinding me to the unseen. Most days, it seemed that I could hardly even catch a glimpse of the unseen, let alone fix my eyes on it. But for Jalpa, she had learned through pain and darkness, to fix her eyes on heaven.

And now, she was there. There was no longer any struggle. Instead, there was eternal glory, all of the time, every moment, in the very presence of God himself. The temporary had finished and the unseen, the eternal had begun. In a moment.

10

THE TURNING POINT

For Jalpa, the temporary had finished, but for me and for her family and indeed for the rest of Nepal, the struggle continued. The monsoon, the living and the political unrest continued, and it continued without her. In Kathmandu, in the middle of the rain, the seven political parties forged an alliance. They forged a common agreement and they began calling on King Gyanendra to restore the dissolved House of Representatives. In turn, King Gyanendra called on the political parties to come for dialogue and to prepare for municipal polls. But they said they would not. Instead, they blamed him for breaching agreements with the people and they spoke out against his methods. They said that while thirteen political leaders were still under house arrest after the takeover they would not come for dialogue. And as the arguments went back and forth, it seemed that the mood on the streets was also gradually changing.

In Dhulikhel, many of our friends who had initially supported the royal takeover seemed to be slowly changing their minds. Some of them began to look back over the previous five months and wonder how anything had progressed. They talked it over with each other. What if the king had been merely using the Maoist insurgency as an excuse to systematically dismantle the democratic system? What if he was all talk and really had no intention of handing back power to the people? What if he was merely using the political backdrop to craft an autocratic rule for himself? And while our friends in Dhulikhel talked, the papers reported the death toll. In Bharatpur, a crowded passenger bus hit a land mine and 36 civilians died. In Dhangadhi, a Maoist attack killed six policemen and their families. In Shantinagar, 250 youth were reported to have been abducted by Maoists. And so it went on.

Then, in July, we began to see glimpses of a new twist. Instead of calls between the political parties and King Gyanendra, there were now calls between the political parties and the Maoists. The seven political parties began calling on the Maoists to shun violence against civilians. And in response, the Maoist chairman himself, Prachandra, ordered a halt to all violence against unarmed people. He went on to express commitment to the seven-party alliance and he applauded the parties' decision to boycott municipal elections.

It seemed like a new thing, yet it was early days. The seven parties went on to list a whole set of conditions before they would talk with either the Maoists or the king. The leaders were still under house arrest, the news on FM radio was still banned and the EC suspended millions of Euros in aid for education. Any resolution seemed impossible.

And during all this, it rained and rained and then it rained again. We read the papers and we listened to the conversations in the bazaar and we sat and stared out our windows. The corn grew and grew until it was taller than all of us. We wrote story after story. We did maths and maths and more maths. Around us, the soggy clothes hung on every possible piece of furniture, in vain attempts to dry. The clouds seemed to come in wisps across the valley until they also sat forlornly in the middle of our living area, waiting for a change in the weather, waiting for a change in the story.

Every now and again in those four months, through sheer desperation, we forced a change in the scene. One day in August we took a taxi to Kathmandu and revelled in the sights and sounds of the big city. We visited friends and heard the sounds of other people's voices. We found a hotel with a pool and we swam and laughed in the rain. We went to the big shops and to the children's library and then we ate steak and chips for lunch.

While we were dipping our chips in tomato sauce, I again cast my eyes over the daily paper. And then I read it more closely. One of the leaders of the seven-party alliance was sounding very positive.

'Once an environment of confidence is built between the alliance and the Maoists, we can bring an end to the king's authoritarian rule once and for all.' I kept eating my chips and thought about it all. I had always understood Nepal's monarch to be a revered figure. In their eyes he was a reincarnation of a Hindu god and worshipped as one. Yet, here in black and white was a deliberate calling for an end to his rule.

Then I thought back to the royal massacre that had occurred in the palace four years earlier, when Crown Prince Dipendra had apparently gunned down almost every member of the royal family, including his father, King Birendra. That year, the Nepali people had moved into a state of shock at the loss of their beloved monarch and they had then watched in silence as his brother, the current King Gyanendra, was crowned. I wondered at the progression of it all. Somehow, as the monsoon poured down all around us, it seemed like the invisible enemy, that had always been the Maoists, was changing shape and looking more and more like the king.

While I was wondering about the transformation, we finished our lunch and took the taxi home again – and it all began again. It rained for a very long time. Then on 1 September the Maoists announced a three-month unilateral ceasefire. It was the first time that there had been a ceasefire in Nepal for two years. We sat up and looked hopeful. But the palace responded by saying that they would not reciprocate the truce. The

National Human Rights Commission urged the palace and the army to reciprocate, but the king issued a statement saying that the Maoist truce was just a ploy. The Civil Society formed a Committee on Ceasefire Monitoring and they also urged the king's government to reciprocate the truce. But nothing happened. It continued to rain. We continued to write stories.

Then, on the very last day of September, we woke up and drew the curtains. The sun was once again lighting up the Himalayas, peak by peak. The clouds had gone and the distant view had returned, in spectacular array. We had made it through one hundred and ten days of rain. We couldn't believe it!

More visitors arrived and we once again threw ourselves into the life around us. We biked and we ran and we shopped and we sat under the pipal trees, talking to everyone who passed by. And the best thing was that while we were doing so, we stayed dry. The clothes went back into the cupboards, the mould disappeared, and in our garden the corn was harvested. Out in the terraced fields in Dhulikhel the rice was harvested and our Hindu Nepali friends began preparing for their two major Hindu festivals of the year, Desai and Tihar.

But for us, the most significant event happened in November. In November of 2005, we sat on the flat roof of Dhulikhel hospital and watched our first batch of physiotherapy students graduate. They were the first nationally trained graduates to receive qualifications in physiotherapy from DMI. One thousand Nepalis found their plastic seats and the ceremony took seven hours. But we weren't counting. We were sitting back and reflecting on the journey that had brought us there.

As we sat there, we even tried to explain it to the boys. We told them about our dream that had begun twelve years earlier. We told them about our years working at Western Regional Hospital in Pokhara in the nineties when there were only two Nepali Bachelor-level physiotherapists for the entire country.

We told them about being part of the original training idea. And then about our years back in Australia and the challenge to return in order to teach on the course. We told them about the effort that that had involved – as if they hadn't noticed. Then, we told them that we were finally there, sitting on the ridge, on the top of the mountain, as it were, watching the very first graduates receive their certificates.

I'm not sure that the boys really understood the concept, but in explaining it to them, we saw it more clearly for ourselves. And in seeing it, we breathed in and made the most of every single moment. We looked back at the stage and saw the ten beaming faces: Hom, Ajit, Subarna, Makhmali, Sudarshan, Yadov, Binayak, Prathana, Birochan and Sabina. Their white coats shone and they held onto their gold envelopes with both hands, some of them staring down at the emblem of Kathmandu University and others of them staring out at the crowd, catching the eyes of those who loved them.

I think we felt as proud as they did. After the ceremony, we had them all back to our house for a chicken *dal bhat* feast. The music echoed across the valley and so did the laughter. The students blindfolded each other and spun around and around shouting out Nepali numbers until they collapsed on the ground. The girls dressed in their most colourful *kurtas* and danced in the courtyard. We hung piñatas from the wooden swings in the back garden and they took it in turns to bash them with the stakes from the tomato plants until the sweets flew in every direction, all over the terraces.

But it was not long after graduation that we thought we should make a decision. We needed to decide on the best month for us to return to Australia. Our commitment to Nepal was for a three-year term which would conclude in the following September. However, we also needed to take the boys' education into account, at the same time as the worth of the work we were involved in.

On the one hand, Darren's involvement in the physio course was extremely satisfying. We had just seen DMI's first physiotherapy graduates. After twelve years of waiting and praying and preparing for the day, we had actually sat there and watched them receive their certificates. Then, in the coming weeks, we watched them as they all found jobs, half of them out of the Kathmandu valley, which was amazing in itself. Makhmali even initiated a non-government organisation in a remote area to service destitute and impoverished women. It seemed to us that the students had not only picked up the techniques to be competent physiotherapists, they had also picked up the compassion to serve the poorest of their people. In a society where receiving a certificate is the gateway to affluence, it was an incredible answer to prayer. And behind our first graduates, came the students in their first, second and third year, also eager to learn as much as they could. It couldn't have been better. And at the point of making the decision there was no Nepali physiotherapist to take over Darren's teaching workload.

As well as that, our relationships within the community and the church had grown. They no longer felt as tenuous as the mist that crept in from the mountains. They had long moved on from the days of fleeting eye contact and the semblance of a smile. They had become long and involved conversations, evoking tears as well as laughter. Their faces had become as distinct and imprinted in our minds as they had once been blurred. Their history had become, in part at least, our history. And we had become, in part at least, something of who they were.

Darren had also been working hard on translating Bible study booklets into Nepali. Along with one of our old Nepali friends from Pokhara, he had almost completed study booklets covering Galatians and Ephesians. They were almost ready for printing. The Wednesday night group in Dhulikhel was growing and changing, ever keen to study more of God's word.

I had become re-involved in a Bible correspondence course, now based in Kathmandu. The course had already reached 320,000 students, a remarkable landmark, especially given the impact of the civil war on the postal system. It all seemed to be evidence of God's hand upon his people and his ministry in Nepal. Even the church across Nepal showed remarkable growth – allegedly the highest recorded growth rate of the Christian church in any country in the world at the time. As well as being remarkable, it was also evidence of a task not yet completed. It was a pull to keep us there.

But on the other hand, Stephen was due to turn 11 in June 2006. His personal and spiritual growth had shot ahead, leaving me in awe at times, but his social contacts in Dhulikhel were fairly limited. Although there were always Nepali children at the soccer field to play with, it wasn't the same as sharing a connection with someone who inhabited the same worldview. Losing our Tuesday afternoon treats with our Irish friends had probably touched him the most. As well as this, the Sri Lankan and Indian families had also returned to their respective countries. To deal with our lack of expatriate relationships, and to cheer ourselves up, we had created a new and revised system of spending every holiday with other expatriate families, spending blocks of time at the INF mission school in Pokhara and visiting Kathmandu more often.

In the end, it was great, but it wasn't enough. It was lovely but it wasn't a long-term solution. We knew that we had to, once again, understand the season. We had to revisit the thoughts we had as we arrived in Nepal for this second term: 'We feel like we have a window of time,' we had tried to explain to our friends and relations back in 2002. 'It's not really that long, it's three years at the most, but it's probably enough for now. After that, Stephen will be preparing for high school and we think we'll need to be back in Australia.'

In December 2005, as the chill returned to Dhulikhel, we gazed at the fresh snow on the Himalayas and knew that we were right. As a family, we needed to return to Australia. Stephen, and therefore all of us, needed to go home. So, we set the date for June 2006, just six months away. That way, we would be back in time for the boys to do six months of school in Australia before the long Christmas break at the end of that year.

At the same time as making the decision, I began to look through the new year's calendar that had arrived in the mail and I even started to pencil in dates, trying vaguely to imagine being in another country. I circled the date that we might move back into our home in the Blue Mountains and tried to address the feelings within me. Even though I knew that the decision was right, part of me didn't really want it to be right. Part of me wanted to stay and part of me wanted to go. Part of me wanted to do both.

One day in December, we were talking through the issues with the boys and moaning about all the things we would miss.

'Our garden and all the fun we've had in it – building all the forts.'

'My tree house,' said Chris.

'That's not just your tree house!' argued Jeremy.

'It is so! The one in the orange tree.'

'All my friends,' Stephen butted in to solve the argument.

'Frazer and Ashleigh and Tim and Daniel.'

'And the long-tailed birds,' said Jeremy.

'And the monkey.'

'What about the motorbike and going over the jumps on our hill?' asked Darren.

Everybody yelled in agreement, in sheer delight at the thought and the feel of the jumps, until our laughter turned slowly into a question.

'But what about the deaf lady?' asked Chris. 'Who will she laugh at, if we're not here?' There was a silence while none of us could think of an answer to his question. The gecko popped his head out during the pause.

'I'll miss home-school,' said Stephen. We all turned, smiled and agreed with him. And then we went back upstairs to carry on with home-school.

11

MAY THE NATIONS BE GLAD

In making the decision to leave in six months' time, we had in some ways already moved into transition. But on the other hand, we still needed to live fully where we were. We still needed to focus our attention on the place where God had put us and on the people around us. By December, some of the new third-year physio students had formed a Christian group on campus. They were led by an enthusiastic young man who had been trained as a Hindu priest and then been converted in his twenties through the witness of a Christian at his local hospital. He turned out to be a gifted evangelist and he soon had a group meeting weekly to pray and study the gospel. Quite a few of his physio friends came along to enquire and to hear the gospel. Then, with Christmas approaching, they had a great idea. In a town that knew nothing about the reasons for celebrating Christmas, they would hold the first ever Christmas programme at DMI.

It was a great idea but it was met with some fairly stiff opposition. 'This is not a religious institution! Why should Christians be allowed to hold such meetings?'

The threats seemed to be significant, even hinting at violence and the group began to get cold feet. They ended up holding a meeting to decide whether to go ahead or not. Darren came home that day and told me all about their conversation. Apparently, at the point where they were going to

give up, someone had read from Luke 1 where the angel said
to Mary, 'Do not be afraid.' Then, someone else had read from
Genesis 26 where the Lord said to Isaac, 'Do not be afraid.'
Then, someone else had read from Deuteronomy 1 where the
Lord said to Moses, 'Do not be afraid.' Then, someone else had
read from Isaiah 44 where the Lord said to the writer, 'Do not
be afraid.' And so it went on through Jeremiah, Matthew, John
and Acts. 'Do not be afraid, for I am with you.' And they
decided to hold the Christmas programme.

On the day of the programme, 150 students turned up to
hear what the Christians had to say. They settled into their
seats, ate the free *khaja* and tried to make sense of what they
were hearing. Halfway through the programme, when a lady
began to share her testimony, some of the students at the back
began to laugh openly. But she turned to them and smiled,
'You may laugh at what I am telling you today, but this is what
I have to say to you, I am telling you the truth. This is my story
and this is what Jesus has done in my life.' She continued to
speak and the students closed their mouths and listened.
Afterwards, thirty of them came to the front to talk to the
Christian students. They wanted to know more about Jesus:
who he was, his authority, his claims and his reason for dying.
There was no further opposition and the group on campus
continued to grow.

In the same week as the Christmas programme, a further
event marked the end of that year. It was very significant. The
seven political parties reached an official agreement with the
Maoists. The agreement had twelve points and it hinged on
the Maoists giving up their armed struggle and committing
themselves to multiparty democracy. It also hinged on the parties not going back to join the king. In the political realm, there
was hope again. In the paper the following day, Kofi Annan,
the UN Secretary-General welcomed the understanding and
encouraged the Maoists to extend their unilateral truce

beyond December. He also urged the palace to reciprocate the truce.

The following week, the Maoists did extend their ceasefire by one month and it was lauded by the parties and the international community. The king, however, did not reciprocate the truce, still stating that the truce was merely a tactic for the Maoists to meet their crooked objectives under the pretext of a ceasefire. So the days crawled on and by the first week in January, the papers were reporting the Maoists' new battle cry, 'To Kathmandu.'

In Dhulikhel, we were feeling the effects of being in transition. After the image of sitting on top of the mountain at graduation, we now seemed to be on the downhill run. Around us, the slope was increasing. I noticed it the most in home-school. For nearly all of January and February that year, home-school was fantastic. It actually began to work at a day-to-day level in the way that I had always imagined it could work. Somehow, it had transformed into what it was meant to be. Jeremy, at almost five, was able to join in for the majority of the morning and we found ourselves studying ancient history through making model Viking ships and hearing stories of far away lands. Each day, as we lay outside on the home-school rug and soaked in the stories and the sun, we also seemed to soak in the appreciation of a chapter in our life that was time-limited; a chapter that was, in fact, not going to last forever. I noticed also that I no longer needed to moan aloud during the afternoons for more patience. I noticed that, mostly, I had patience. Was I able to put more of myself into the task, knowing that the end was in sight? Is that what happens on a downhill run? Perhaps, but even on a downhill run, there are dangers, there are struggles, there are unexpected twists lurking just up ahead.

In early February 2006, we were walking through the town to church as we always did. Fresh green growth had begun to replace the barrenness of a Dhulikhel winter. Groups of Nepalis were gathered at various points, chatting by the tailor's, waiting at the statue, haggling over bananas. It seemed, at first glance, like an ordinary Saturday morning in Dhulikhel. But it wasn't. There was a strange, indefinable heaviness in the air. It swirled, invisibly, around the townspeople as they came and went. It collected in denser waves, almost palpable, at the meeting points. It was simply, but intangibly, there. Tension.

After months of deliberations, King Gyanendra had called for district elections and they were set to take place on the coming Wednesday, 8 February. Both the Maoists and the political parties had vowed to disrupt and boycott the process. The Maoists called a week-long general strike, with heavy threats of violence. Somehow, people felt in their bones what was coming. They felt it, but they wished that they didn't. We felt it in a transmuted kind of way. Not our own, but owned nonetheless. There were more eyes darting around, there was more twitchiness, there was a certain sharpness in the pitch of the voices. As we moved through the bazaar, there was an ache in our own bellies.

We carried the ache into church. We sat down in our corner and rearranged our bags and our Bibles, fiddled around with our jumpers and hats, appearing busy but merely letting the ache settle. In front of us, Praju was slowly standing and moving forward to begin the church service. She reached the front of the room and turned around and faced us. She rearranged her pink headscarf until it sat neatly on her dark hair, then smiled and looked down as she read from Psalm 67:3–4:

> May the peoples praise you, O God; may all the peoples praise you. May the nations be glad and sing for joy, for you rule the peoples justly and guide the nations of the earth.

There was a pause as the words sank in. May *all* the peoples praise you. I sat there and thought to myself that on a day like that Saturday in February I'd have quite understood it if the psalmist had said, 'All you nations, all of you except for those of you who are in civil war. If you're in civil war, facing a week of riots, attacks and violence, you don't have to praise. You can sit very quietly and pray.'

But the Psalm didn't say that. And on that Saturday morning, nobody wanted to sit still. The entire room stood up, joined together and sang praise song after praise song. Their voices merged and echoed around the concrete building until the very walls danced. The sounds of worship floated out of the windows and into the bazaar. Children in the streets raised their heads to find a reason.

The reason was simply this: in a civil war God is still God. He is still worthy of our praise and we *want* to praise him. Our very being cries out with a deep reverence to the Almighty God. We can't sit still. There is something about civil war and all the horrors that go with it that makes us turn to him even more. And what other way is there to turn to him?

That morning in church, we turned to him in honour and praise, for he is who he says he is – the Lord of all.

12

MY ONLY REFUGE

I'm one of those people who can get absorbed in the task of making a house into a home. It occupies me, heart and soul, for the initial weeks after a move, usually to the detriment of other, more minor considerations, like food to eat or clothes to wear. I try to create cosy little spaces everywhere I can and then fill them with objects of meaning. Then, once created, the home becomes my refuge.

Sometimes, I kid myself that all this activity is for the benefit of Darren and the boys. But it's not really – it's for me. No matter what country I'm in I do it, with whatever help I have available. In Dhulikhel, I covered the whitewashed walls with wall hangings and pictures, I redid all the curtains in burgundy and put photos of our loved ones everywhere. They stared down at us from the walls of the kitchen, the lounge, the school room, even the stairwell.

As soon as the walls were covered, the curtains redone and the cushions matching in a vague kind of way, I knew that I was at home. It didn't matter about the lack of hot water or the power cuts or the rat in the pantry, I was at home in my refuge and it was, for us, a safe place. The heavy maroon gates that enclosed our three town houses meant that we didn't get too many unwanted visitors, so as soon as we stepped inside them we felt safe in our own little world. We could lie on the soft grass at the front of the house and read stories or play with

Lego. I could sit wrapped up in our quilt with my back pressed up against the pillows of our bed and gaze out of the windows at the Himalayas. Darren and I could sit together on the back porch with a cup of tea and watch the boys make forts, climb the plum tree and try out their newly constructed bows and arrows. We could be together, safe in our refuge.

We knew that disastrous things were happening everywhere else in the country. We knew that there were riots in Kathmandu, bombs in Nepalgunj and shootings in Nagarkot. We even knew about the sounds of gunfire at our closest army camp – but it was never in our house. In our house, everything was still, everything was quiet, everything was safe. That's how it is in a refuge.

It wasn't that we were naïve. We knew that we should be very careful and we knew that we should have contingency plans in place. We had plenty of them. We might not have had an address in Nepal but we had a GPS reading of the house and we had it recorded at the Australian embassy. The INF security team had assessed our house for safety in the event of gunfire. The downstairs toilet, being the only room with all internal walls, was deemed to be the place to gather in the event of a Maoist attack. We would laugh as we imagined all five of us squashed into 120 centimetres square for hours and hours, playing 'I spy'.

'I bags sitting on the toilet!' Stephen would say.

'Then I'm sitting on you!' Darren would counter.

I would merely laugh and try not to let my mind imagine a situation that would cause us all to spend an evening in the toilet.

The evening of 9 February began in the same unremarkable way that most other Thursday nights began. Darren shepherded the boys upstairs for their bucket baths while carrying a hot kettle of freshly boiled water. I stayed downstairs to clear away the remains of our spicy sausages and rice. I peered under the table and discovered piles of it in the gaps between the old brown lino. I sat down on one of the chairs and picked out the bits of rice that had embedded themselves in my socks. I noticed the quietness of the night and I enjoyed it.

From upstairs, I could hear the sounds of running water and Jeremy's voice echoing around the tiles, 'My bucket's too cold! Can't you get me some more hot!' I heard Darren's voice respond much more quietly, staying calm. 'There's no more hot water, Jeremy, just get in . . .'

Moments later, the sounds of splashing mingled with the voices. An occasional rise in tone signalled the arrival of the shampoo, but the mood stayed calm and quiet. I turned off the downstairs lights and joined them all for bedtime stories under the blue quilts that had provided comfort all their lives. It was warm and we felt sleepy. We wrapped ourselves in stories of security and protection. We reminded ourselves of God's care for us as we drifted off to sleep.

About four hours later, I woke suddenly and the darkness surprised me. I lay without moving and wondered what had woken me. I listened to the stillness until it was broken by the sounds of the second bomb. The force of it made me shudder. I reached for Darren. His body lay in the quietness of sleep but I saw that his eyes were wide open. His stillness was deliberate, listening. The next bomb was only moments away. I felt every muscle tense, ready to respond. Ready, but unsure. My eyes moved around the room, wanting to know where the danger came from but seeing only a darkness that gave no clues.

'What should we do?'

I thought the words more than I said them. I heard them whisper across the inside of my head. Speaking them would have broken the silence. I held my breath until the next bomb exploded. It sounded as close as the next room. It was followed by the sound of gunfire that echoed across the valley and from above our hill.

We knew the questions: Is it steady and rhythmical like a game of darts? Or is it more haphazard, with answering fire? We'd always been told that it would be easy to tell.

In the stillness of the night, it wasn't. I lay there silently, listening to the echoes, thinking that the stiller I was, the more I would be able to trace the source and the rhythm of the fire. But I couldn't. The stiller I was, the more I flinched with each new sound.

'Should we be in the toilet?' I whispered.

'I don't know,' Darren replied.

Getting to the toilet meant creeping into the boys' room, waking them and carrying them downstairs to the toilet. Should we risk that? The only rule with gunfire that I really understood was the importance of keeping flat. An upright target is much more easily hit than a flat one. We were upstairs, but at least we were all flat. And in between the exposure of upstairs and the safety of downstairs was the stairwell which contained a large window in direct line of fire with the army camp. And there's another good rule; whenever there's gunfire, keep away from the windows. What should we do? Stay lying prone in our warm beds or fiddle around upright, targets for an indefinite time period, in order to get to a safe place, in order to get to the toilet?

We stayed still. We lay flat and still and wide awake for the entire night. We flinched at every sound. We redefined tension. We gripped at pockets of air, as if in thin air lies security. We counted thirteen bombs and a steady stream of gunfire. All night long we debated whether we should risk the stairwell. All night long we prayed for the kids – and they stayed asleep.

Many hours later, as light was creeping into the world, Darren went in to check on the boys. He bent over Stephen's bed and noticed that he was awake and peering out of his window.

'Dad – what's that helicopter hovering around up there for?' he said.

It was the very first time that my refuge became a place of danger, the very first time that I questioned the depth to which I had apportioned my home as my sanctuary.

Darren went to work that day and discussed the situation with his students and the other lecturers. Apparently, overnight the Maoists had attacked the army bases at neighbouring Panauti and Dhulikhel as well as various government offices. As they sat chatting and eating their *dal bhat* in the hospital tea shop, a crowd began to form near the stone wall that separated the hospital from the paddy fields. Staff members and students pushed together and then began to point in horror as a dog dragged the remains of somebody's body across the street to the area below the stone wall. It was horrendous.

Four weeks later, the questions of refuge came again, in ever increasing intensity. By then, of course, it was March and spring had come to Dhulikhel. Spring in Dhulikhel is short-lived but very beautiful. It was most evident beneath our plum tree. The blossoms weighed so heavily that passers-by were unknowingly adorned with its bounty. The feathery white petals shone and mingled with the pods of fresh peas growing beneath them. The wind blew and spring let the world know that beauty had not departed.

That afternoon I had gone next door to have a cup of tea and an Anzac biscuit with Margaret. She carried two cane chairs outside and we sat in the sunshine and drank slowly. We watched the boys through the hedge as they picked fresh peas under the plum tree. We saw a mongoose scurry up her orange tree.

'Isn't this just delightful,' I said.

'It couldn't be more peaceful,' she replied.

We took one more sip and then her phone rang. Sharp and piercing, it interrupted more than our conversation. She left her tea and went off to answer it. I stayed in the cane chair, watched the boys and caught fragments of her conversation.

'Oh, I see . . . Well then, yes . . . thanks for telling us.'

After some time, she came back through the glass doors waving her hands and speaking quickly.

'That was the administrator at the university. He's just had a tip-off from the Maoists. They're planning a bigger attack on Dhulikhel and it could be tonight. They plan to approach the area over our hill and they're concerned that our houses will be in the firing line . . .' She paused to let her words catch up. 'So, we need to get out. It's not safe. He says we need to evacuate for an indefinite time period and he's sending a vehicle over at 5 p.m. to collect us. He says we should try and be ready.'

I looked down at my watch. It read 3.30 p.m. I looked at Margaret and we both glanced briefly at our cups of tea. There was no time. The moment for drinking tea and enjoying the springtime had passed. It was time to panic!

'Boys!' I shouted. 'Come inside! We need to leave and go somewhere else. Can you collect some things?' I was already crawling through the hedge and back into our own garden.

Stephen came up through the terraces first and looked confused, 'What things?' he said.

'I don't know. Anything at all. Anything you want.' My words fell out so quickly that even I didn't make sense of them.

'What do we want?' asked Chris.

'Underwear, socks. Whatever. I don't know. I don't know what you want.'

I raced up the stairs, grabbing objects as I went and wishing that the go-bag was stocked, thinking briefly that perhaps I wasn't the queen of packing after all.

Jeremy knew what he wanted: 'I want blue bear. Can I bring him?'

'Yes. No. If you can fit him. Somebody get the toothbrushes!'

We dashed in different directions, tripping over each other and forgetting how to count to five. I ran into the boys' room to grab their clothes but couldn't remember whether we already had socks or underwear. I forgot their hats. I glanced frantically around the schoolroom, hoping that something worthwhile would jump out at me. Two maths workbooks and an English text and a pencil case did. I stuffed it all in and ran back down the stairs, colliding with Stephen on the way.

'Where are we going?' he asked.

I put a calm smile on my face and tried vainly to slow down my speech.

'Somewhere else. Somewhere nice and quiet, so that we don't hear any awful noises.'

'Why, Mum? What awful noises?' asked Chris. I paused again, mid-flight.

'Well, you see – the Maoists might come tonight and they don't want us to get in the way, so we might just move somewhere else.'

'Are they going to blow up Dhulikhel like in *Age of Empires*? asked Stephen.

'I surely hope not,' I replied, weakly, 'but I still think it will be nice for us to live somewhere else for a while.'

Darren arrived home from work to the general confusion and added his pile of belongings to the mound at the front door. Moments later, we heard the jeep park out the front and we all piled in, trying not to look backwards, trying not to wonder how long it would be or what our home would look like when we did come back. Should I have taken all the photos off the walls?

The jeep steered us through the streets of Dhulikhel. We passed the army camp and I caught sight of faces that I knew. These were the men who marched up and down our hill every morning. These were the men who stopped to smile at us and greet us, who watched the boys play cricket. These were the men who were the targets. Had anyone told them? I turned my face away and tried not to cry.

Instead, inside the jeep, we swapped stories and the rumours that we had overheard. Apparently, the Maoists had been seen congregating in the fields behind the hospital, ready to attack. The phone lines had also gone down, but nobody quite knew why. We watched piles of men getting off the buses at the bus stop and tried hard not to imagine their intent.

Our jeep turned the last corner and we alighted at the university guesthouse. The concrete steps were cold and unyielding. The walls were bare and empty of meaning. I looked around me at the beige bedspreads. It was not cosy, but it was safe. It was out of range of the firing line. Or so they said.

I dumped the bag on the floor and walked out onto the balcony while the boys argued over which mattress they could claim. Outside, the sky was darkening and the lights were coming on in the distant hills. I looked back in the direction of our home. I could just about pick out our roof amongst the trees that covered the hillside. And I looked up at the hill over which the Maoists would come. Then I wondered what would stop them coming over the next ridge or via the next village. I drew a firing line in my mind between the ridge and the place where I was now standing. When bullets are fired – where do they end up?

It took a very long time for sleep to come that night. It might have been the spicy *dal bhat* that we ate for dinner. It might have been the adrenaline that had brought us there. It might have been the ache that sat deep inside us. But when sleep did come, it was restful.

I woke in the morning and my very first thought was – the absence of war. I was thankful to the point of tears for the stillness of the night. There had been no noise of gunfire and there had been no explosions. We were thankful.

We managed to find some toast for breakfast and then a table and some chairs in the empty room next door. It was just

the right size for home-school, so we said goodbye to Darren
as he left for work and then gathered around the table as we
always did for assembly. I prayed, demanded quiet and pulled
out our Bible. The previous month we had decided to read
through the Psalms during devotions every morning. We were
up to Psalm 27, so I read it very slowly that morning:

> The LORD is my light and my salvation –
>   whom shall I fear?
> The LORD is the stronghold of my life –
>   of whom shall I be afraid?
> When evil men advance against me
>   to devour my flesh,
> when my enemies and my foes attack me,
>   they will stumble and fall.
> Though an army besiege me,
>   my heart will not fear;
> though war break out against me,
>   even then will I be confident.
> One thing I ask of the LORD,
>   this is what I seek:
> that I may dwell in the house of the LORD
>   all the days of my life,
> to gaze upon the beauty of the LORD
>   and to seek him in his temple.
> For in the day of trouble
>   he will keep me safe in his dwelling;
> he will hide me in the shelter of his tabernacle
>   and set me high upon a rock.

The most surprising thing was that the boys were listening.
They were all as still and quiet as they'd ever been in home-
school. We were all listening – to the voice of God to us, on that
March morning, high in the Himalayas and far from our home.

He was with us. Though war should break out against us, he was with us. Though an army should besiege us, he was with us. And because he was with us, I could be confident. But what exactly could I be confident in? What did it mean that he would keep me safe in his dwelling? What did it mean that he would set me high upon a rock? Did it refer to my physical safety?

I looked around me at the bare walls above the table and faced the answer being 'no'. When I put my confidence in God it doesn't mean that I won't experience gunfire. It doesn't mean that I won't find bullet holes in the morning. It doesn't mean that I won't know tragedy, perhaps to the worst degree. But in that day of trouble, I will know his presence and I will gaze upon his holiness.

I took a deep breath in and realised that God was giving me something more than just a head knowledge kind of confidence. In that moment, he was giving me a deep sense of his peace and his presence. There really was nowhere I could go that was apart from his presence.

And then as I sat there that morning I realised that, in the most part, I had put my confidence in almost everything *but* the Almighty God. I hadn't normally admitted to it; I had just done it very quietly. I had put my confidence in my home, my husband, my profession, my own ability to problem solve. But mostly, I had put my confidence in my home. I had thought that my home was my refuge. I thought that the walls could keep out the enemy and provide us with a place of safety. I thought that I could be confident as long as I was within my home.

But that was before we were evacuated from it in March 2006 and fled from the threat of war. On that morning, as we sat in the bare guesthouse and reread our psalm, I realised that it was the first time that God *alone* was my refuge. My home had become an unsafe place to be, but in losing my home, I had found refuge in God. And I realised that in that moment, I exchanged the theoretical understanding of his presence to the comfort of the tangible.

13

A DESTINATION

The first night in the guesthouse was quiet but the threat of Maoist attack was still there. It hung like a heavy blanket over the town of Dhulikhel. Day after day the townspeople gathered in the market-place to share their concerns and line up for the daily paper. They stocked up on rice and lentils and simply waited.

And so did we. For the first three nights, we stayed at the guesthouse. For three nights in a row, we went to sleep fearful and woke up thankful, thankful again for the absence of bombs and gunfire. Every now and again we became so absorbed in a story or a race up the stairs that we even forgot about the threat. We just enjoyed the moment. Then we would look around us at the sink in the corner of the bedroom and all our belongings in one bag on the floor, and we would remember. We were not at home.

After three nights, the administrator of the university reissued his advice. 'You must not go back to your home. The attack is still to come. Please be careful.'

We looked around us again at the single room. The mattresses on the floor seemed to be taking up even more of the available space. The boys were beginning to behave like tigers in a locked cupboard. We needed to be able to stretch our arms out. So, we decided to relocate once again.

We hopped on the local bus and moved to the INF transit flat in Kathmandu and enjoyed being able to walk between four rooms. We enjoyed and we waited. Stephen took tennis lessons. Chris and Jeremy played on the flat roof above our rooms. I hung out washing. Darren commuted the 30 kilometres to work at DMI each day. And we all waited for permission to return home. We waited for the all-clear. It never came.

Instead, the urgency just seemed to slowly reduce. The attack seemed less imminent. The commands were less serious. The mood was more relaxed. The questions, though, were more tortuous. Should we risk going home? Knowing what we now knew, could we manage it? Could *I* manage it? Could I return to my refuge, knowing that it no longer was my refuge and knowing that it could happen again? I wasn't sure. I debated it. I debated it with myself, I debated it with Darren, I debated it with God. I debated it with anyone who would listen. And I still wasn't sure.

Then one morning I came up with something. 'All right,' I said to Darren as he hung up the phone, 'here it is. *If* John and Margaret move back in and if they have their satellite phone and *if* the *chowkidar* (the Nepali who kept an eye on the townhouses) moves back in – then I'll go home.'

I smiled to myself, knowing smugly that the odds were on my side. The likelihood of the three occurring together was next to nothing. I knew it and Darren knew it. But he said nothing. He merely agreed.

The very next day, John and Margaret returned to Dhulikhel – with their satellite phone – and the *chowkidar* moved back into his quarters. 'Bother . . .' I thought to myself.

We repacked our hastily assembled possessions. The correct number of undies and socks found their way back in to the bag. The toothbrushes were reclaimed from the bathroom. The maths and English textbooks were gathered from the desk that had become the new school room and we moved back home.

Once again, we travelled the road through the outskirts of Kathmandu, past the rivers and the rubbish heaps, through the straggling bazaars and then up and out of the valley. Once again, we were surrounded by tractors and lorries, motorbikes and strangely oblivious cows. By March 2006, we knew the road as well as we knew our terraced back garden. Some weeks it even felt like an extension of our terraced back garden. Some weeks we no longer even needed to look out of the windows to know and to feel the scene before us.

On that day in March, though, I stared through the taxi windows, alert for signs that would somehow give me more information, information that had perhaps eluded me up until that point.

Darren, aware of my twitchiness, kept telling me to calm down. 'Everything's fine,' he kept saying, 'of course it's fine.' As well as repeating his lines, he also seemed to be cleverly avoiding my gaze. He knew the next lines in the script. So did I.

'How do you *know* that everything's fine?'

'Everything's fine because the Nepalis say that it is. They're the ones that know what's really going on. They live here and they say that it's fine. So, we just take our cues from them.'

He knew I wasn't convinced, so he added one more argument. 'Look, when we get home, I'll go to the bazaar again, I'll talk to lots of people, and I'll go and see Suman. I'll find out what they all think and then we'll have the update. Then we'll know.'

I nodded and relaxed. I watched out of the window as we made our way past the Dhulikhel police station and the bend before the soccer field. I saw Nepali faces that I recognised, women with their loads and children with their slates and pencils. And I slowly eased back into the sense of home.

When we turned the last corner and parked at the top of the hill, our home was still there, intact. The white walls reached high, once again bordering the dark red windows, seemingly as sturdy and as immovable as they had been when we left. Our home; no longer a refuge, perhaps, but still our home. The boys bundled out as usual and raced up the stairs, longing for the blue quilts and the belongings that they had left so hastily two weeks earlier. I left them to their delight and wandered into the school room.

It was still there as well, with all our books left open and poised at a single moment in time that had existed two weeks earlier. Two weeks earlier, Chris had been writing in his story book. It lay open on his desk with the neat pencil lines telling the story, 'When we were having breakfast my tooth fell out.' Stephen had been working on a still-life drawing of a pot plant. It lay on his desk, the shading half-finished, the pencil discarded. Jeremy had been working on smearing play dough all over his desk. It also lay there, discarded. It lay in mounds, dried out and cracked into position, two weeks of airing not having added to its appeal.

I sat down on one of the bamboo stools and thought about it all. It was 22 March 2006. We were due to leave the country permanently on 26 May, just nine weeks away. I stared at the desks and the covered walls and tried to think ahead. We had nine weeks to go. I looked at the calendar and counted the weeks again and it was still nine weeks. Having just effectively skipped two weeks, we were suddenly closer than I thought.

My gaze shifted to the mounds of school work that we had collected over the twenty-four months of home-school. The piles of craft materials and resource books sat dubiously on top of the cupboard, wedged beside the model aeroplanes and the Viking ships, teetering out of their allotted space. I looked at the blue and white stripes on the Viking sail and knew that I should begin to deal with it all. If, for some reason, we had to evacuate again, the nine weeks would quickly disappear. So I pulled out the four blue barrels and began to pack.

I packed for so long that it grew dark and the *bijuli* went off. Chris poked his head round the door and asked why I was sit-

ting there in the dark, with only one candle. And more importantly, what was I doing with his Viking ship? I ummed and
ahhed and evaded the question for a while. Then I volun-
teered something.

'I thought it might be a good idea to pack some of our
things.'

'But we've only just come home!' He stared at me. 'Do we
have to move house again?'

'No – not as far as I know. I just thought it might be a good
idea to start sorting through our things. Just in case . . .'

'In case of what?'

'In case we have to leave again in a hurry.'

'Oh, then I'll get you another candle. It's way too dark in
here.'

He went off down the stairs and while he was gone, Darren
poked his head through the door. He also asked why I was sitting there in the dark with only one candle.

I said that I was packing. He came into the room and sat
down on the other bamboo stool. And that was odd in itself.
He doesn't normally sit down to think. I looked at him while
he spoke.

'Packing might be a good idea,' he admitted. And then I
stared at him.

'What do you mean?' I said.

'I've just got back from Suman's . . .' he paused and looked
at the pile of maths books in my hands. 'I'm thinking that
maybe we should put the spare mattresses on the floor in the
kitchen tonight – there's more room there and it would be
safer.'

'Safer,' I repeated, slowly. 'Safer, in case of what?'

'Well – just in case it gets noisy again tonight.'

I stared at him. 'What did Suman tell you?'

He glanced away, he evaded. He had good reason to. He knew
that I was worried enough as it was and any more information

might not be helpful. Instead, he went off to arrange the mattresses and to pray with our neighbour John. I kept sorting, aware
of a new urgency.

I sorted for three days and three nights as the shadows from
the candlelight flickered around the school room. While the
shadows flickered, the night sky stayed silent. The mattresses
in the kitchen stayed there, but we didn't need to use them. No
unforeseen noises intruded into our home or into our
thoughts.

On one of the candlelit evenings, I looked at the calendar and
noticed that it didn't completely stop at the end of May. It did-
n't fall off the end of a cliff or move into a non-existent vacuum.
Dates were beginning to form in June, July and August – dates
in another continent, in another home, in another life, a life
where we could go out in the evenings. It was a strange, almost
incomprehensible thought. And it flickered, like the candles.

But as I packed, I began to think about destinations and
about the deliberateness of life when we know that we have
one. As I worked towards my given date, I began to be much
more systematic as, every day, the date grew closer.
Sometimes steadily and sometimes in a panic, I dealt with the
things that I needed to, in order to leave well.

During that week in March, I spent a whole day with Saru,
the pastor's wife, in her little shop by the bus park. We prayed
and chatted and drank *chiya* and the heat of the boiling glass
seeped into my fingers as the smell of fresh spices seeped into
my being. I tried to prolong the moment, feeling the hardness
of the wooden stool and hearing the noise of the bus park and
seeing the face of my friend as she spoke. I listened to her soft
words with a new intensity, aware of the loss to come.

The next day, I handed over all my Sunday school materials
to her daughter, Sanju. She stared at them, delighted. She even
fingered the cane container that they all sat in. 'We could use
this for the manger in the Christmas drama!' she cried, her

eyes dancing with delight at the sight of something so useful.

And then the next day I went to Srijana's house and handed over piles of children's clothes and pencils for school. Again, we drank *chiya* on the mud step of her home and watched the scene in front of us. We watched the children as they climbed to the top of her mango tree. We watched the buffalo as it nosed up against her two little black goats. We watched the chickens peck around our feet for scraps of husked rice. As I watched, I closed my hands tightly around the metal cup which contained my *chiya* and wished that I could do the same with the scene before me. I didn't know then, how quickly it would depart. And I didn't know then, quite why I was doing my leave-taking so early, but somehow I knew that I had to.

While we were thinking about our departure to Australia and preparing for our move across countries, we also took an excursion to a smaller and yet infinitely taller destination: Everest Base Camp – the top of the world. Having spent hours in home-school studying the route, we had also made plans to walk there in early April. For years we had made plans and for years we had thought that it was good timing. Not only would our boys be as old as they could be and therefore more able, but we had also heard rumours of a nationwide *bandh* for a whole week in early April. It sounded serious. So, we decided that being up in the Himalayas, away from the smog and the vehicles and the political turmoil, would be the best place to be.

And we were right. As the Twin Otter negotiated the last Himalayan ridge and then slowed to make its landing on the tiny, inclined runway at Lukla, we leaned forward in our seats. We stared out of the windows and took in the majesty of the snow-capped peaks that surrounded us. We saw the forests that covered every ridge below the snow. We stepped out of the plane and breathed in the freshness of air that had blown straight in from the snow.

Lukla is a small village, high in the Himalayas. It's the starting point for all the treks in the Everest region so it does a good trade in lodges, food and trekking equipment. We found some wooden benches in a sunny spot, ordered boiled eggs and *chiya* and pulled out our maps. The maps, having already been well-studied in home-school came alive now that we were actually on them. We found ourselves on the maps, we found the route and we found the destination. We found the reason to get up each morning.

There is something about trekking in the Himalayas which is terribly freeing. It reduces life to its bare and manageable components. You wake up in the morning and order porridge and *chiya*. You dress, eat when it arrives and repack your bag. Then, you walk. You walk up hills and down hills, past yaks with bells and over forested mountains. You walk past signs in Tibetan and over high suspension bridges. You share the walking with traders and tourists, porters and friendly children. As you walk, you watch where you're going, you dream, you make up stories for your 5-year-old, but mainly you walk. You stop for *dal bhat* at lunch time and then you get up and walk again. You walk all afternoon until you get to the day's end, then you eat *dal bhat* again and you sleep. Then it all begins again the next day and the next and the next, until finally you arrive at your destination point.

Trekking is all about destination. Whenever you stop anywhere, whether it's for the view or the photo that will transform the moment into a memory, someone will be bound to pass by and ask you, 'Where are you going?' 'Where have you come from?' 'How much further?' 'How long does it take?'

You become so focused on the destination that, for the short trekking period, there doesn't seem to be any other question in life. There are no other questions and there are no other answers. It's merely kilometres and hours and *dal bhat* stops until you get there.

By day three, our trekking party (that consisted of the five of us as well as Darren's father Dennis, our Australian friend Richard and our friendly porter) had rounded the last hill and arrived, happily, at Namche Bazaar. The town is built into the rounded side of a hill and, from a distance, light reflects luminously from the blue-tinged roofs and the mountains that tower over the town. From a distance, the bells ring out and the sounds of the town invite you in. We settled ourselves into three small rooms at the 'Camp de Base' and moved into the dining area to order *dal bhat*.

It was warm. The red glow of the fire flickered on the timber walls. We found some comfortable seats by the fire and watched out of the windows as the wind began to whip up the snow on the mountains. Clouds hovered over the peaks and merged with the snow, reminding us that the weather also affects the destination.

While we waited for our *dal bhat* and the boys found their packets of cards and their journals, other groups also entered the dining area and made themselves at home. We heard the shuffles as they rested their heavy packs by the door and removed their jackets. We heard their accents as they checked the menu and inspected the Snickers bars in the glass cabinet at the back of the room. They joked with each other, before the questions became more serious.

'How far are you going?' The Canadian man rearranged his scarf around his red polo fleece and waited for the answer from the German who had just entered the dining room. The question appeared casual, nonchalant, when they both knew that there was only one answer that counted: 'The summit.'

It was, after all, April in Namche Bazaar. April in Namche Bazaar meant that every serious climbing party was spending the mandatory few days there to acclimatise. For climatic reasons, they all needed to reach the summit by the end of May or in the first week of June. There is, in fact, no other time of year when an Everest ascent is possible. So, if you want to meet potential climbers of the highest mountain in the world, you simply sit quietly in the corner of a dining hall in Namche Bazaar in April. You leave your book open on your lap, you gaze out of the window and you listen.

The Canadian party sat down to our left and began to eat their macaroni cheese. The leader of the party grilled them in a loud voice over whether they were all getting enough protein in their diets. Then he pulled out a pulse oximeter from his bag and began to pass it around to his team mates, encouraging them, between mouthfuls, on their scores.

'Oh . . . 96.' He pressed the button to restart while he swallowed. 'That's very good.' He nodded at the blonde girl who sat beside him and then he turned his attention back to the German who had settled on the next table.

'Is this your first attempt?' he asked in a voice destined to be heard.

'Yes,' replied the German, more softly, 'and yours?'

'No.' The Canadian moved into his element. 'We attempted last year but were prevented by weather patterns. This year we have daily three-way-satellite weather reports.' He smiled and somehow sat up straighter. 'We're prepared and ready. You might be interested to know that we're also attempting to be the first husband and wife team on top of the seven continental peaks – the tallest mountains on each of the seven continents.' He introduced his blonde wife proudly to the man, who looked suitably impressed. 'We married on top of the Antarctic peak and we've climbed all the others in the last two years, but we've left Everest till last.'

I smiled to myself as he began his description of the way they had strolled to the top of Kosciuszko the previous year.

I returned to my book, while the Canadian turned to some new arrivals in the dining hall. The conversation began again, the filtering, the sorting out of the sheep from the goats. The divide ran down the room, neatly and cleanly – those on their way to the summit and the also-rans who were merely going to Base Camp or the Gokyo Lakes. At Namche Bazaar, they wore the same gear, they ordered the same food, but their eyes were on a different destination.

And then there was us. We were somehow separate, a breed that they couldn't quite understand. Every now and again they tried to. A new arrival, a tall Israeli man who was clearly out of breath from the last hill, stared at Jeremy as he played outside in the newly fallen snow.

'He didn't walk all the way here did he?' He turned to look at me, wanting some reassurance.

'Umm, yes – actually he did.'

'Oh,' he tried to catch his breath before he turned to Stephen. 'So, how far are you going?'

'Base Camp,' said Stephen calmly.

'Oh,' he said again, turning to the menu while he re-worked his next question. 'So, where have you come from?'

'Lukla,' replied Stephen, dealing out another round of cards to play rummy with Richard.

'But – where is your home?' asked the man, clearly confused.

'Dhulikhel,' said Stephen, looking up only to answer. The man was at the point of giving up.

'But what country?'

'Nepal . . .' Stephen paused only for a fraction. 'Or Australia – actually, kind of both.'

Perhaps we were the breed without a home, without a clear beginning but, like them, we definitely had a destination. The next day we got up early and walked to Khumjung, the town famous for the school that was established there by Sir Edmund Hillary. An hour or so and several snow fights later, we settled down at a lodge, our hands wrapped around mugs of hot chocolate and our eyes wrapped around the view. Right in the centre of the panorama before us sat the face of Everest, emerging clearly from the plateau of a ridge immediately in front of it. To its right and left sat the snowy faces of Ama Dablam, Lhotse and Nuptse. In between the three lay the Khumbu glacier, the largest glacier in the world.

'That's where we're going tomorrow,' said Darren pointing to the route which trailed around Tengboche and then followed the glacier. Our eyes followed his outstretched arm in wonder.

Chris pulled out his map from his pocket and traced it with his finger. He knew that, in fact, he would be staying with Jeremy, Dennis and me in Namche Bazaar but he still wanted to know the route that the others would take. Despite the fact that he was not going himself, he wanted to know about their destination. He wanted to dream.

As I sat there, warming my hands on my mug and trying not to drink the chocolate too quickly, I thought about destinations. We had become intent on the journey. Stephen knew each day how many kilometres he had covered and how many he had to go till he reached Base Camp. He knew how many metres he had covered in altitude and how many more he had to climb till he reached Kala Patar, the 5,545-metre peak that they aimed to climb above Base Camp. He knew, mostly, that he was further along than he had been the day before. He took encouragement from that fact. Although he knew that the climb would get harder and the breathing more difficult, he knew that he was closer.

And as I thought about it, I realised that it was another part of the truths that God was teaching me. As I stared out at the physical path ahead, the parallels with my spiritual journey spoke to me. If in my walk with God I also have a destination, then right now, today, I'm further along the path than I was yesterday. I sat there and thought about how easy it was for me to not only forget about heaven, but also to forget that I'm closer today than I was yesterday. Instead, I seem to think that the path is some kind of playing field that I merely run all over, dodging here and there and changing the game and the direction as I feel like it, waiting for the bell to ring. It seems so easy for me to mistake the path for a field. As I sat facing the tallest mountain in the world and thinking about the route to its summit, I was reminded that the route I walk with God is also a path, a path with both a beginning and a destination – and the destination is important, it's the only answer that counts – heaven.

The following day, our party split up and we waved good-bye to Darren, Stephen and Richard. We stood at the steps of our lodge and watched the sway of their rucksacks as they disappeared around the next bend. Stephen's retreating figure seemed to be so much smaller and more fragile than the other two. I was silent for a while, feeling the chill of the breeze and trying not to think about frostbite and altitude sickness, headaches and hypothermia – and all the other dangers that lay around the bend, beyond my viewpoint. Chris pulled urgently at my arm.

'When will we see them again? Mum! How many days? When will we see them again?'

I picked him up and hugged him. 'Only nine, I hope.' I buried my face in his thick polo fleece and felt the beat of his heart. 'That's not many, is it?'

By the time we had turned around and walked back the way we had come, up hills and down hills, past yaks and over ridges, and arrived once more at the sunny lodge in Lukla, that was already three days. Along the way, the cherry blossom floated across our path and Chris and Jeremy collected bundles of it to mark their way. The more they gathered blossom, the more they walked. And the more they walked, the more I enjoyed the journey. I walked slowly and noticed the geraniums growing out of old rusty oil tins placed in front of the lodges. I listened to the yak bells as they echoed across the valleys. I smiled at the porters as they rested their loads. I looked upwards and said goodbye to the Himalayas.

And then three days later in Lukla, Chris came rushing out of the bathroom in our lodge. 'Mum! It's got two taps! There's really truly hot water. Hot water! Can we have a shower?' It was a fitting way to mark the arrival at our temporary destination.

14

THE BIRD SONG

On Monday morning, 10 April, Chris, Jeremy, Dennis and I flew in a Twin Otter from Lukla back down to Kathmandu. There was nothing out of the ordinary about the flight. We rolled down the incline that made up the tiny runway and we were in the air before we even had a chance to unwrap the boiled sweet that lay beneath the Yeti Airline sweet wrapper. Jeremy spent the twenty-minute flight playing with his cotton wool ear plugs. Chris spent the twenty-minute flight watching the pilot and wondering whether he too should be a pilot when he grew up. He wasn't entirely sure one way or the other. The twenty minutes passed by in contemplation and we found ourselves once again emerging from Kathmandu airport, at precisely 11 a.m. And that was when the extraordinary things began to happen.

The first taxi driver I approached looked away while he demanded a flat fee of five hundred rupees to take us to Thamel, the tourist area of Kathmandu.

'*Panch say rupiya!*' I repeated in Nepali, horrified. A standard metered taxi should charge around one hundred and fifty rupees for that particular journey. I stared at him. Perhaps he thought I was a naïve tourist, ripe for the picking. So I repeated my request using more complex Nepali grammar, the kind of grammar that can only be picked up through months and years of living with it.

But he didn't budge. He didn't care who I was. It was five hundred rupees or nothing. It was all very odd. So I turned to the next taxi in line and had almost a replica conversation. Then I noticed that he was already pulling out, empty. Indeed, so were they all. That day, of all days, the taxi drivers were in a hurry.

Annoyed, I turned to Dennis and the boys. 'For some reason, all the taxis are asking five hundred rupees just to take us to Thamel. It's crazy. Let's go and find a taxi on the ring road.'

So we hauled our packs back onto our tired shoulders and trudged down the street that connected the airport to the main road. The humidity felt like a blanket on my face and the sweat pooled beneath the straps on my shoulders. Jeremy yelled out, demanding to be carried, having just walked all the way from Namche Bazaar to Lukla. I said something inane about the road only being thirty metres away.

Thirty metres and more complaints later, we reached the main road. It was the same road that it used to be, except that it wasn't at all. Normally, the ring road is the busiest road in Kathmandu. Normally, it's a cacophony of noise. Taxis and *tuk-tuks* and motorbikes swerve around the cows and the men carrying loads. They announce their presence to the bicycles with the whole musical spectrum of bells and horns. Normally, it's impossible to cross the ring road. Normally, we stand on the side for what feels like hours, hoping that we won't get mowed down just by watching. We wait for ages, turning our heads back and forth, and thinking that a break in the traffic is about as likely as a break in the noise. Normally, we end up waving down a taxi, which neatly avoids the challenge of having to cross the road.

On the 10 April, our world seemed to shift. We reached the ring road and it was deathly quiet. We looked to the right, and there was not a solitary vehicle for as far as our eyes could see. We looked to the left and it was the same. There were no bicycles, no *tuk-tuks*, no tractors, no taxis, no motorbikes and no lorries. There was silence – and that very silence, that we had longed for in days gone by, was alarming.

We looked to the right again and realised that there were also no people. There were no women with loads and no men with vegetable carts. There were no children playing with their *chungis* by the side of the road. There were not even any people sitting outside the houses that lined the road. There was silence.

'Mum! Where are all the taxis?' asked Jeremy.

'Mum! Where are all the people?' asked Chris.

Before the questions could be answered, a well-dressed Nepali appeared on the street behind us and began to wave frantically. 'You must go inside! You should not be out with these small boys.' He waved even more manically in the direction of Chris and Jeremy. 'It's very dangerous! There's a day-time curfew and there are police everywhere. Go back inside!'

'Oh–' I attempted to smile calmly at the others. 'Now that would explain the lack of taxis.'

My eyes darted up and down the street again, searching for signs of life – and there were none. The man beside us was beginning to fidget, obviously keen to disappear in the direction from which he'd come. Go back inside. I repeated the words in my head. Go back inside. Inside where?

While I was engaged in the inner, pointless conversation, a very large taxi appeared silently behind us, ferrying tourists to Thamel. I hesitated for only a moment at the five hundred rupee fee and then we all jumped in, squashed against each other with our bags pressing up against our noses and our eyes fixed on the scene. We sat and stared out of the windows, saying nothing.

The pocket dictionary defines silence as being the absence of sound or noise – stillness. On that day in April, silence was a vacuum, an emptiness in a place that had been designed for noise. It was an unseen danger hidden just out of sight. The shop shutters were closed, the curtains were drawn, the bleating and bell-ringing and touting had ceased. The people, the inhabitants of Kathmandu had gone, disappearing into the vacuum. All one million of them. Silence was something eerie, almost palpable lurking in the place where laughter and movement had been. Silence was a city under daytime curfew.

Right through the middle of that silence, our taxi moved. The driver was in a hurry. He told us that he had a special pass to ferry tourists from the airport all day. The quicker he got us to Thamel, the quicker he could get back to the airport. He pressed down hard on the accelerator and screeched around corners that would normally have been blocked by a myriad of motorbikes and *tuk-tuks*. He laughed at the feel of his engine, unhampered for the first time by other vehicles.

The only problem was that in place of vehicles, there were soldiers in tanks. As we careered at lightning pace around each corner we spotted another group of them, guns pointing straight at us, waving us down. Our taxi driver stopped with a screech and the soldiers surrounded our vehicle. They leaned through the windows, so close that I could smell their sweat. They frowned and grilled the taxi driver in loud, incomprehensible Nepali – and then they waved us on. It happened at least six times before we made it to Thamel. Each time, the same heavily-armed soldiers in the same deserted streets. The same questions and the same answers. It was as if we were the only habitants of the city, the only ones fleeing to safety while the others had already vanished. Somewhere.

In Thamel, we were quickly let out at a corner which would normally have been buzzing with rickshaws and the sounds of trading. Ordinarily, we would have struggled to dodge the build-up of waste in the gutters as we avoided the oncoming traffic. Not that day. We stepped out of the vehicle and felt the silence. It mowed us down. We stared at the closed shutters and the empty streets. We were momentarily disorientated. Without the open shutters of the Walden's bookshop and the Weizen bakery and the little jewellery shops and the sari shops, how could we orientate ourselves? My feet did a full circle before sensing the direction of the Tibet Guesthouse, less than two streets away.

We reached the shelter of the hotel foyer and it felt like the arms of a long-lost grandmother. We stepped inside and the colours of the rugs sprang to life. We heard the murmur of voices in the hall and we noticed the smile of the lady on the desk. We smiled back and booked into our standard four-bedded room on the second floor. Number 209 – four beds, a hot bath and cable television. While she made the booking, I looked around me and noticed the sign that hung below her desk, 'Nationwide curfew from 10 a.m. Please stay inside.'

I was inside and so were the boys. Inside was familiar and safe, almost a refuge. People gathered, spoke to us and then carried our bags upstairs. People moved around normally, they spoke on the telephone and read the papers. Inside, we could pretend that outside was normal as well.

But it wasn't. After we had deposited our trekking gear and tried vainly to make some sense of what we'd just travelled through, I found the day's version of the news, the *Kathmandu Post*. I read that Nepal had moved into day five of a nationwide indefinite daytime curfew and general strike, initiated by the political parties and the Maoists and targeting the king. Demonstrations were taking place across the country and there were reports of pitched battles with the riot police. Two protesters had been killed in Banepa and three others had been critically injured.

I looked up from the paper and let my eyes rest on the walls of the hotel room. I wondered how long we would be stuck there. I wondered how long it would be before the roads opened again and we could return to Dhulikhel.

Chris and Jeremy turned on the cable television and discovered *National Geographic*. They immersed themselves in a story on great white sharks, wondering why we didn't have any in Nepal. While they were happily absorbed, I unpacked our trekking bags and took a critical look at the contents: three sleeping bags, three sets of thermals and an equal numbers of polo fleeces. Numerous pairs of thick smelly socks and trekking shoes that needed airing. Apart from the trekking clothes, which were unwearable in the steamy heat of Kathmandu in April, we had one pack of cards and a book each. The books had already been read and reread. We also had our three journals but they had quickly lost their appeal after the destination had been reached. If we were stuck indefinitely in the hotel room, how would we stop ourselves from crawling up the walls?

Maybe we wouldn't. I had a shower. I felt the heat of the water on my tired shoulders and I began to relax. I was aware of the light coming in from the streets through the tiny frosted window. The boys were quiet. And as I became more attuned to the absence of noise on the streets, I became aware of a new noise. Birds singing. *I could hear the birds.*

In the heart of Kathmandu, on the second floor of the Tibet Guesthouse, you don't normally hear the birds. You hear the ringing of bells and the bleating of horns, you hear men shouting and the fizz of pressure cookers. You hear motorbikes screeching and the banana lady dropping her price, but you don't normally hear the birds.

As I relaxed in the shower, they sang – and I listened. It was sweet and it was beautiful and the more I listened, the louder it seemed. I even found myself trying to copy the bird call and beginning to wonder what sort of bird it was. Then, after a while, another thought came and this was it: the birds must have always been there. It was more that in the usual hubbub of the street I'd never heard them. As I reached for the towel and dried myself, I wondered how much I had also missed of God's voice in the hubbub of my life. It took me a curfew and a silence to realise it.

The next morning, we were all up bright and early, to the sounds of – nothing. We stared out of the window at the void and slowly moved into what was to become our curfew routine. Firstly, Dennis went downstairs to reception and enquired about curfew hours. Nobody knew.

'Well – how are we supposed to know which hours we should stay inside?' he asked.

'You wait and see,' replied the lady on reception.

'We wait and see until when?' he questioned.

'Until they tell us,' she said.

'But when will that be?' he probed.

'We don't know,' she told him.

Dennis and I looked at each other. We could go out for an indefinite time period but we had to be back inside at an unknown definite time, to avoid the curfew. We didn't know when the unknown definite time would be and we wouldn't know until it arrived. That meant that we didn't know how far away we could venture, because we didn't know when we would have to be back. Then, amidst the list of unknowns, we looked at the boys. They were running up and down the hotel stairs and delighting in the sound of their voices as they echoed off the stairwell.

We went out. We went to the Weizen bakery which was pretending not to be open, but the discerning and hungry amongst us discovered that a side gate was secretly open. We ordered porridge and banana *lassis* (yoghurt drinks). We read the paper. It was day six of the extended *bandh* and protest programme.

King Gyanendra and his government were threatening to take tougher action against the protesters and anyone else that broke curfew. All road travel in the country was impossible and most domestic flights were cancelled. All banking services had ceased until further notice. Prices of consumer goods were again skyrocketing. I put down the paper and looked at my watch. It was approaching 9 a.m.

'Do you think we'd better get back?' I asked Dennis.

'Yes, I think so,' he replied, 'it might be a 9 a.m. curfew.'

As we prepared to creep back out of the side entrance, we caught sight of a crowd accumulating at the end of the street. They seemed to be shouting and waving clubs. They were coming in our direction. Dennis was already out. We had to stay close to him. I grabbed the boys' hands and tripped over my feet as we tried to catch up with him. I yelled out to him but I couldn't hear my voice over the noise of the crowd behind me. We stumbled on and caught up with Dennis at the paper shop. We all ducked inside its secretly open door. As we peered back out of the door, the protesters swept past us, their shouts increasing but still incomprehensible to us. I felt the strength of the crowd. And I felt within myself the over-whelming instinct for self-preservation.

As their shouts reduced in volume and my heart rate returned to normal, I straightened up and pretended to look at the maps in the shop window. I called to Chris and Jeremy and they showed me some postcards of tigers that they'd found. I had a good look at them before saying that we should proba-bly head back to the hotel. I wasn't in a hurry. And I made sure both ends of the street were completely clear before we crept out.

Back in the hotel I realised that we'd been reading from the gospel of Mark that very morning to prepare ourselves for Easter. And we'd been reading from Mark chapter 14 where Peter hid in the crowd and denied his Lord, not once, but three times. That very morning, I'd been hard on Peter, not under-standing why he had failed to speak up. I hadn't realised until then the terrible strength of self-preservation that exists in the midst of a hostile crowd.

But two hours later, after hiding in the paper shop, I knew. I had felt the same struggle, the same self-protection – and the crowd wasn't even after me. But as I sat in the hotel room I asked myself the question – what if they had been? What if they had stormed the paper shop and demanded the arrest of all Christians? What would I have done? I looked out of the hotel window and whispered the answer so that no one would hear – 'Stayed hiding.'

I'm pretty sure that I would have stayed cringing in fear behind the rack of posters. And as I imagined it that morning, I understood the amazing grace of God once again: that he should so love someone like me and that he would give his only Son so that I would not die but have eternal life. It seemed once again, astounding.

15

SEPARATED

Downstairs, the notice was out again. 'Nationwide curfew from 10 a.m. Please stay inside.'

We stayed inside – and we set the pattern for the coming days. First of all, I washed the smelly socks and underwear in the tiny sink in the bathroom. Then, we lay on the beds and watched *National Geographic*. We learnt about the habits of lions in the wild in Africa. Then, we played rummy. Then, we took the lift up to the rooftop restaurant. We sat on the wooden seats and stared out at the city under curfew. We watched the Tibetan flags blowing in the breeze and counted the solar panels on the hotel roof next door. We made up complicated gymnastics routines using the poles that were holding up the roof. We discovered the sudoku puzzles in the *Kathmandu Post* and we noticed the way that the Himalayas caught the light as they soared above the valley. We commented on the lack of smog that was making them visible. We thought that it was funny. The mountains were out but the people were in.

We kept our curfew routine up for five days. And during those days, the gymnastics routines turned into mad obstacle chases and volatile arguments. The lions on the television transformed themselves into caged boys in the hotel. The Tibetan flags began to blow with discontent and frustration. One morning, feeling desperate for another outlet, I decided to risk a trip across town. I had good reason to. Friends of ours on the other side of town had been looking after our laptop computer while we were in the Everest region. If I could only get across town and retrieve it, I would be able to send and receive emails. And that would give me something to do!

I left the hotel early, feeling alert and twitchy. Once again, I didn't know what time the curfew would be enforced. There seemed to be a range of possibilities – anything from 8 a.m. to 11 a.m. It was impossible to guess, and if it was an early start I could well be caught on the wrong side of town, unable to return to the boys. But I was desperate. So I left complicated instructions with Dennis and the boys in the event that I was stranded somewhere and then jumped into the first taxi that I could find. I didn't even question the price.

As we made our way through lanes and deserted shopping markets, I listened to the driver. He told me all about how hard it was for him. He told me about the little room where he lived with his wife and parents and children. He described the single bed and the kerosene burner. He told me about being stuck inside it for a week.

I tried to picture it.

'So – what have you been doing all week?' I asked.

'Well, I've been sitting and then I've been sleeping and then I've been sitting again and then I've been sleeping again.' He looked across at me. 'What else can I do?'

I couldn't think of anything. 'It must be terribly boring,' I said.

'It is,' he agreed, 'but that's not the worst bit. While I've been sleeping, I've been losing five hundred rupees a day. I can't get outside to drive the taxi, so that means that I can't earn any money and I can't feed my family.'

I looked at him and his face embodied the frustration of the people caught in the middle of the conflict. The ones who could do nothing were the same ones who bore the conse-quences of the curfew. Up until that point they had done what they had been told and they had not protested the appalling conditions. But for the first time in that taxi I saw glimpses of a new movement, a new level of frustration that might lead the country to a new place.

With those thoughts in my mind, I jumped out of the taxi and raced down the alleyway to retrieve my laptop. Then I flew back across town again, aware of a new determination. I not only arrived back at the hotel in time but I also committed myself to understanding the movement from the viewpoint of the people.

I relieved Dennis from the spectre of dire contingency plans and then pored over the day's newspaper. I read about the dozens of protesters who had been critically injured in unprovoked firing by Armed Police Force personnel. I read the voices of concern from the US, the EU and the UN. I read of the determination of the political parties to continue the agitation regardless of the palace's increasingly harsh measures to control it.

Then I started to notice the shift. On day ten of the nationwide curfew and violent protests, the Lawyers' Association joined in the demonstrations. The numbers of protesters across the country were increasing daily. Thousands of people, including women, children and the elderly, were defying the curfew in order to increase the pressure on the king. For the first time in the history of the conflict, the pro-democracy movement was swelling from the ground upwards. I felt the swell and the momentum, the power of the people.

Then, as I checked the dates on the papers, I realised that it was time for Darren and Stephen to return from the Everest region. While I had been washing socks and counting solar panels I had been trying very hard not to think about altitude sickness and hypothermia. I had been answering Chris's questions regarding where they would be now without allowing myself to imagine them not being where they should be. Or maybe I had just been pushing the thoughts away like sand on a picnic rug. When the days began to drag, Chris's questions became more complicated. 'What will they do if their flight arrives after curfew?' and 'What if there aren't any taxis?' and 'How will they know where we are?'

'It will be alright.' I kept saying. 'They'll know where we are. They'll hear the news and they'll guess.'

For once, I was right. The morning that their heads peered around the hotel door was about as exciting as it could possibly get in a week defined by curfew routine. We turned off the television and discarded the game of rummy. We jumped up and hugged them, breathing in the air from the mountains that still clung to their clothes and hearing their stories in a garbled, tumbled-out fashion. We heard about the yaks that had stampeded them halfway up the mountain. We heard about the swarm of bees that had somehow become trapped in Richard's hair. We heard about the view of Everest from Kala Patar, the 5,545-metre peak above Base Camp. We heard that it was just like God had been drawing pictures in the sky: shades of blue and purple on a Himalayan backdrop. The destination had, indeed, been worth the journey.

Some hours later, when the stories had subsided, we swapped news. We explained what we had been doing sitting inside a hotel room for five days. We tried to paint the pictures of the routine and, in doing so, we realised that we were actually strangely fond of it. We couldn't wait to take them up to the rooftop restaurant and share it all with them. But they weren't so impressed.

'How long are we going to be here?'

'We don't know.'

'Can we go home?'

'Not right now.'

'But when?'

'We don't know.'

It takes time to move into a curfew routine. I thought that it would be much more fun being stuck in a hotel when we were all together. And it was – it was a lot more fun but it was also a lot more noisy. There were more bodies to entertain and there were more questions to evade. There were more sibling conflicts to negotiate and there were more caged lions to deal with. There was also more compound anxiety as we all wondered what would happen next.

Richard was also stuck. He found another room in the hotel and wondered how long it would be before he could return to his wife, Penny, and their two children who were in Pokhara, two hundred kilometres away. We met him for dinner that night and tried to imagine the infinite number of separation scenarios across the country.

'There must be thousands of people stuck in the wrong place,' said Stephen with his mouth full of noodles. 'Imagine! What about all the people down in the Terai (the flat area of Nepal bordering India) who were on their way to work or back home or visiting their relatives. None of them can travel anywhere either. There must be stuck people everywhere, all over the country!'

Somehow, it felt better to remind ourselves that we were merely part of a large group of stranded people, not individual cases. Easter Sunday came and the curfew remained early. We toyed with the idea of attending the International Church on the other side of the city, but the sounds of the void once again reminded us that it was impossible.

Not put off, we pushed the hotel beds together and made our own church. The beds became four comfortable pews as well as the pulpit. The boys were happy to sit still because Dennis had just produced the lure of all lures: Easter eggs all the way from Australia. There is nothing better for boys under curfew. We tore our eyes away from the eggs and read from Ephesians chapter 2:

Remember that formerly . . . you were separate from Christ, excluded from citizenship in Israel and foreigners to the covenants of the promise, without hope and without God in the world. But now in Christ Jesus you who once were far away have been brought near through the blood of Christ. (Eph. 2:11–13)

And it seemed to give us a whole new slant on the concept of separation. We now knew vividly how it felt to be separated from our home and all our things. We knew how it felt to be stranded and unable to go anywhere. We knew the gradual build-up of frustration and the search for unworkable solutions as the desperation increased. But God knew how it felt to be separated from all of us, his own children, by sin. Not for nine days, but for generations and generations. He knew the pain of seeing us far away. He knew the desperation of a Father who would do anything to bring us back together again. And in the end, his unthinkable solution was the blood of his own Son, Jesus. And it worked. We who were once far away were brought near, for all time, never to be stranded again. The good news was very good that Easter. And so were the eggs.

But while the heavenly separation had been dealt with, the separation enacted before us on the streets of Kathmandu was worsening.

16

BEHOLD HE COMES

While we sat eating chocolate eggs, we also checked our emails. We read that the American Embassy was now actively encouraging all its nationals to leave the country. Other embassies were advising 'non-essential' people to leave. Two hundred people representing various development agencies had just been arrested while staging a sit-in protest over human rights, peace and democracy.

On day fourteen of the political protests across Nepal, Dennis flew home to Australia. He left the hotel very early that morning, not wanting to risk being caught in a curfew again. That was fair enough . . . he had used up all his excitement allocation on our previous race across town through a curfew. We stood and watched his taxi disappear around the corner and then dragged our feet back inside the hotel. Nine days inside a single room had wearied us. We didn't even care who won the next game of rummy, much less bother about what was up next on *National Geographic*. We simply didn't care. We stared out of the window and wished that it was us on the plane. Planes were not bound by four walls. Planes were free.

But we couldn't get on the plane and fly to Australia because all of our belongings were in Dhulikhel. And we couldn't return to Dhulikhel because all the roads were still cut. In fact, three bombs had been found that very morning on the road to Dhulikhel. Even if we could return, we couldn't live there, because the entire water supply to the town had been cut off. And that was a story in itself.

At some point during the protests the residents of Banepa, a town five kilometres away from Dhulikhel, had apparently staged a large demonstration against the police killings of the two protesters from Banepa earlier in the week. The demonstration was large and vocal. Tyres were burnt and bricks collected on the roads. To increase their voice, the neighbouring towns of Panauti and Dhulikhel had been called on to swell the numbers. Panauti responded with vigour but apparently Dhulikhel did not match the numbers. So, in true score-settling style, Panauti decided to teach Dhulikhel a lesson.

Many years earlier, a water supply system had been put in place using the run-off from the river that flowed straight through Panauti in order to service the town of Dhulikhel. The story is vague but it seems that Panauti did not come out of the deal very favourably. So, when the scores were once again on the table, the residents of Panauti decided to cut a hole in the pipes that led to Dhulikhel. That would teach the residents of Dhulikhel a thing or two.

I think it did. For all the weeks that we were stuck under curfew in Kathmandu, the residents of Dhulikhel stood queuing up at a local tap that had a separate water supply to the main pipes from Panauti. They then teetered home with their full *gagri* (water pots) on their heads or sitting in their *dokos*. Mind you, that was only when they were allowed out of their houses, in the non-curfew moments. If nothing else it was all getting even more complicated.

So, instead of moving home or moving anywhere on an aeroplane, we moved across town. Once Dennis had safely reached the airport, we decided to move back across town and settle into the INF transit flat, to wait. It was the same flat that we had taken refuge in during our evacuation in March and, for that very reason, it immediately felt like home. As we hauled our trekking bags up the stairs and unlocked the door, we felt huge waves of relief. It even smelled like home. Once inside, we practised walking between the four rooms and we laughed at the way it felt strange to take more than five steps at a time. We could even run!

The first thing that Stephen and Darren did was to move most of the furniture to the side so that they could hit the tennis ball up against one wall. The first thing I did was to recreate the school room. It didn't even matter that we had no school work with us. We could always pretend. As I dragged a table across the room and found a clock to place in its centre, I smiled at myself. The clock stared back at me, smiling also. It was my feeble attempt to bring order into a disordered life. Strangely satisfied I went upstairs and stood on the flat roof looking out over the city.

And it was as if the city was burning. From where I stood, plumes of brown smoke rose in every direction and met on the skyline. The smell of burning rubber filled the air and assaulted my nostrils. The shouts of demonstrators carried from the nearby ring road and became a vague cry against a regime that was no longer wanted. I leaned further out against the railing and could see groups of people congregating between the buildings and the bazaar areas. I listened and watched, aware that the nation's history was unfolding before my eyes. I knew that it was history, but I didn't know how it would end – and neither did any of us. And that was the thing that kept me fidgeting, scared, walking up and down the stairs, not knowing whether I was going up or going down or, indeed, whether I needed to be doing either.

In between going up and down the stairs Darren and I dissected the news. The Indian Prime Minister had just arrived in town to speak with King Gyanendra. A total of 2,000 agitators had been injured so far in the demonstrations. In a nearby town 70,000 women, including family members of security personnel, had staged a demonstration demanding absolute democracy. The Newari community, the original settlers in the Kathmandu Valley, had added their support to the people's movement. Every financial institution and government office had been shut down for more than two weeks. Amnesty International had called on the international community to impose targeted sanctions on the king. Although the swell was continuing, no one knew what the king would do next. Some suggested that he would bring in the army or declare another state of emergency in order to control the demonstrations. If that were to happen, we imagined that there might be a break in the strikes and curfews and we might even be able to return to Dhulikhel. But it was mostly conjecture.

The next day was Friday 21 April and the curfew was called from 2 o'clock in the morning and it lasted until 8 o'clock at night – by which time the night-time curfew came into effect. It was an extremely long day. Stephen found a 500-piece puzzle in the flat, Chris and Jeremy played with the Lego. Darren worked on preparing his physio notes to hand over on our departure. I found a book that I hadn't read and in between chapters I went up and down the stairs – ostensibly to hang out the washing on the line on the roof. Or, I could always fold it over so that the wind caught the other side of the socks. By the time I returned from my fourth trip up and down the stairs, Darren looked up from the computer.

'What have you been doing on the roof?'

'Hanging out washing,' I replied.

He stared at me. 'Every time?'

'It takes a lot of concentration to fold it exactly right,' I said.

I didn't tell him that it was much more than that. I needed a task that I could keep under my perfect control. I needed to influence something utterly. If it was just the socks, then that was better than nothing. The only problem was that we didn't have any more clothes to hang out. We were wearing them. I returned to a sunny spot in the flat, stared out of the window and wrote in my journal.

The day came and went and then it was Saturday and the curfew was set to begin at midday. Darren decided to attend a local Nepali church. At 10 a.m. he crept through the back door of the church and merged with the four hundred Nepalis who were already standing in worship and singing at the tops of their lungs. They were elated to be there. The week beforehand, on the Easter weekend, there had been no church services or house fellowships across the entire shut-down country. Instead, the Christian community had begun a week of prayer and fasting for their nation. They were united in their prayer-life, but they also wanted to sing, and so they made up for it that Saturday.

Apparently, they sang and sang. But thirty minutes into worship, a man made his way to the front and announced the news, 'An earlier curfew has just been called. We all need to go home now.'

Darren told me later how the noise level increased as they reached down to gather their bags and their babies. They rearranged their saris and they sang out their *namastes* as they found their *chappals* by the door. They were noisy, but even more than that, they were thankful. They were so thankful for thirty minutes of worship. It had felt like a gift, an unexpected present in a seemingly endless morass of days. They left cheerful but not knowing when they would be able to worship together again.

Neither did I. By the following day, Sunday, the desperation was getting out of hand. In the alleyways surrounding the transit flat lived half a dozen other Christian expatriates. Normally, they would attend the International Church on Sundays, but once again that was impossible. So, in their weary state, they rang around and invited us to join them all for a time of worship and prayer in the second-storey flat down the road that belonged to a British girl.

The curfew had already been announced on the radio. It was 10 a.m. But we reasoned it out very carefully. The flat was only a five-minute walk away. There were no police or army personnel stationed between the transit flat where we were and the second-storey flat where she was. It was a very quiet alleyway. We could stay well away from the riots. And, most importantly – it would be worth it.

I stepped out of the gate that bordered the transit flat and held tightly onto the boys' hands. I looked both ways and saw that the alleyway was deserted. We moved silently along the street and the silence seemed to move with us. Every three steps, I spun my head around, to check if anyone was following us. I watched the shadows at the side of the street and I was acutely aware of the sounds within the buildings. There were none on the street.

We found the designated building and slipped through the gate, relieved to leave the shadows of the alleyway. We made our way up the stairs and sounds of quiet prayer filtered along the corridor. We crept in and each found a spare cushion to join the others who were already kneeling and praying on the floor. As I made myself comfortable, the view from the window reminded me of the reason that we had come. Thick black smoke from the riots trailed across the horizon, the darker patches giving clues to the activity beneath. And the clues mingled with the silence that encompassed us. I couldn't look out of the window and not give way to fear, so I closed my eyes. I silently prayed and I listened to the prayers of those around me. Our prayers reflected our worry and our lack of words. We longed for peace, for changed hearts, for mercy – but it was so hard to see it with our eyes open.

With our eyes closed, though, somebody began to sing the song 'These Are the Days of Elijah', quietly at first until everyone joined in at the chorus. It was not a song of worry. It was a song of triumph. It was a reminder that he, the Lord himself, the God of Israel, will one day ride in on the clouds and that I am to 'behold him'. I opened my eyes, I stared out of the window and for a very brief moment, it was as if I actually beheld him. The actual skyline still held images of fear and demonstrations but it also held a glimpse of the future; the Lord himself coming on the clouds and shining like the sun at the trumpet call. For the first time in my life, I was clearly seeing 'the unseen' – in all its glory. And I lifted my voice to sing.

Monday 24 April marked our fifteenth day of living under curfew, separated from our home, our friends and our belongings. It also marked further developments in the revolution. The *Kathmandu Post* reported, 'The US State Department has ordered all non-emergency US mission personnel and dependants to leave Nepal.'

The same day, the Canadian and Korean embassies followed suit. Then, the aid agencies gave notice of evacuation to their families and we heard via the grapevine that INF would go into evacuation mode the next morning. There were good reasons for the announcements. It was rumoured that the following day, Tuesday 25 April, there was to be the riot to end all riots. Two million Nepalis were expected to be on the streets and their plan was to storm the palace. The king was believed to be bringing in the army.

Nobody knew what the outcome would be but it could only be gruesome. It was time to get out. We fidgeted within the flat. We made phone calls. We found our passports and thought about plane tickets. It was as if we had already heard the evacuation notice within our own heads and were simply preparing to flee. We looked out of the windows and wondered how flights could be booked without any banks operating – without any money.

But then, at the same time as finding our passports, we also thought about all our belongings back in Dhulikhel. We thought about the boys' scrapbooks and the mementos that they had collected of their lives in Nepal: the journals and the photos and the memories, the concrete reminders that we had actually lived in this country which we were about to flee. If we left without our mementos, how would we ever know for sure that we had lived here?

On Monday afternoon we met with Philip, INF's security adviser. He came straight to the point: 'So, you want to get back to Dhulikhel to say your goodbyes and get your belongings?'

Darren nodded. 'We do – if we can – before we have to leave . . .' he paused and looked at the *Kathmandu Post* that was lying open on the floor, the headlines shouting at us. 'If things keep going like this it sounds like we'll all be on that aeroplane soon.'

Philip agreed. 'That's certainly how it's looking. And I've been giving some thought to your dilemma.' He paused and lowered his voice. He rested both his elbows on his knees so that he could look at us directly. 'Tomorrow is going to be the 'big one', the critical day. We don't know what will happen. So, here's my thought. We take the INF van tomorrow at 4 a.m. and we race up to Dhulikhel to beat the curfew. We grab all your things that we can fit into the van. The only thing is that we would have to be back in Kathmandu before the curfew starts. We can't risk being stuck up there. Do you think you could pack up your whole house in half an hour?'

I smiled at the question. Within the bizarreness of the question, I knew what Darren's reply would be.

'Easy,' he said. He lives and breathes optimism. But he still has questions. 'What time do you think the curfew will start?'

'That's the hard bit,' said Philip. 'It could be as early as 7 a.m., so we'll have to be quick. And we'll have to be careful of punctures as well. The streets are littered with burning tyres and broken glass. But then again . . .' Philip smiled at us, 'what's the worst thing that could happen? We abandon the vehicle, they torch it and we walk home. It's only thirty kilometres.'

He paused again while we pictured the burnt-out remains of the little green van and the image of us carrying the boys and our bags for thirty kilometres through riots.

'That's OK,' said Philip. 'We can do that.'

Darren agreed. 'No worries. What do you think we need to bring?'

Philip had already started preparing. 'I've got a large white flag, so I'll put that in. We'll need a satellite phone too – just in case.'

'Good idea, mate,' Darren smiled. 'Just in case.'

The plan was made and the van packed that afternoon. Philip checked that it had enough petrol. While he was out the back with the van, we heard that there was a late change in the curfew times. A window of time that day meant that Darren could risk a ride to Dhulikhel on his bicycle. If he could get up there earlier than us, he could stay overnight and do some packing. He was in the bedroom grabbing his helmet and his bike gear before I had even registered the change in the plan. Curfews are not, and never will be, his favourite thing. Then he was out the door and waving at us while we leaned out of the window catching the last glimpse of his back wheel.

We moved back inside and I tried to explain the plan to the boys. They couldn't believe it.

'You mean we're really getting up at 4 a.m., in pitch black and driving to Dhulikhel? We're really racing the curfew?' Stephen looked around him as if needing a concrete reminder of reality. 'Wow,' he said, 'that's more exciting than Christmas.'

It was so exciting that they couldn't sleep. But that was probably my fault. I should have learnt the rule by then. The earlier you want boys to sleep, the later they stay up. If you try to put them to bed too early, it will actually produce the reverse effect. They stay up later than you do.

At 10 p.m. I put the phone back down and mulled over Darren's words from Dhulikhel. He had described his bike journey home through burning tyres and smoke and roads filled with broken glass. Then he had described our home, a disordered array of belongings. I tried to picture the scene on the road and then in our living room – and couldn't contain the images within my head.

So, instead, I went back to check on the boys. I walked into their room and immediately sensed wakefulness. Stephen was lying in the nearest bed, his eyes poking out above the sheet and staring straight up at the marks on the ceiling, as awake as I'd ever seen him. I sat down next to him and touched his forehead.

'You're awake,' I whispered.

He nodded. 'I keep thinking about how dark it will be. I've never been up at 4 o'clock in the morning before. What's it going to be like?'

'Well dark, yes, and quiet, I hope.' I looked down at the buzzing in his eyes. 'But don't worry, just try and relax. It doesn't matter if you can't sleep – we'll be up in six hours anyway.'

I went to bed and also lay there for hours, not in the slightest bit relaxed. I alternated between checking the alarm clock and staring at the marks on the ceiling, neither of which really helped. I, too, had never run a shoot-on-sight curfew before.

'Quiet, I hope . . .' I said to myself.

17

THE RACE

The alarm clock went off at 3.30 a.m., about one hour after I'd last checked it. I fiddled with it in the darkness, fumbling with it as it fell off the window sill and into the folds of the bed. My hands closed around its hard corners and I squinted as I tried to check the time and at the same time silence the ringing, automatically trying to keep the boys asleep for a few more moments.

My hands then reached for my blue *kurta* that I had left lying on the end of the bed. I slipped it over my head and started fiddling blindly with the tie on the trousers, feeling them rather than seeing them, acutely aware of the darkness and all that might lie within it. As I listened to the silence of the early hours I was also aware of the buzzing within my own head, the hyper-alert state of the instantly aroused, the watchful darting of the one anticipating danger. I found some spare safety pins and pinned on my scarf to either shoulder. Then, instinctively, I moved to the door so that I could check the position of the scarf in the mirror that I knew hung behind the door. I stared into the mirror and the glimmers of a very dark shadow stared back. I couldn't even see my face, let alone the scarf. I smiled at the thought. I had just checked the position of my scarf at half past three in the morning, in pitch blackness. And the feel of the smile on my face was reassuring. It left crinkles in my skin and the feel of them somehow kept the fear at bay, in the same functional way that the pins on my shoulders kept the scarf from slipping all the way off.

I crept out of the bedroom door and tripped over the boys' shoes and socks, neatly arranged in a row where I had left them the night before. I peeped in their door and heard the sounds of their quiet breathing. I paused for a while, staring at the lumps in each bed and wishing that I didn't have to disturb the semblance of peace, fearing that the rest of the day would not hold any more. Still pausing, I checked my watch again and realised that it was time for the van to arrive.

I touched Stephen's shoulder first. He woke instantly, staring at me with large, excited eyes.

'Is it time?' he asked.

'Yes,' I replied, whispering to him to put his shoes on and at the same time turning to wake the other two.

They were much more difficult to arouse. I started putting Chris's shoes on while he was still asleep and noticed how difficult it was to bend his toes in the right direction to accommodate the shoe. As I reached for the second shoe, I heard Philip's voice in the stairwell. I turned around again and told Stephen to run out and join him. Then I picked up Jeremy's sleeping body and held tightly to Chris who was now awake and wondering what was going on. We made our way down the stairwell and into the waiting green van, still whispering, still groping in the darkness.

I had thought that the silence of the city under daytime curfew was eerie. The silence of the city at 4 o'clock in the morning was even worse. I sat in the back on the bench seat with the boys and I felt myself cringe as the engine turned over. I wanted to duck and hide. The van crept out of the gates that surrounded the transit flat and turned into the deserted lanes. Once again, I kept myself alert, twitching and turning my head for signs of danger. My eyes were wide as they watched for movement or signs of the army. What if the soldiers heard our vehicle and shot, out of panic? What if somebody saw our headlights and suspected that we were trouble – demonstrators set to incite the masses? As I allowed myself to imagine the possibilities, I looked down at the boys. In the dead of night, our pale skin and blonde hair was no longer the protection that we had taken for granted in the daytime. In the darkness we were unrecognisable, we were the same as everybody else. I put my arms around them and we slipped further down into the seat.

The van crept down the last incline and approached the ring road. From our windows we could see huddles of people beginning to congregate along both sides of the road. We could see men on bicycles silently appearing from around the bends and joining the huddles. We couldn't hear their voices but we could feel their anticipation, their intent. Philip had been right. It was indeed the day of the 'big one', the riot to end all riots. In some ways it felt better, watching the people and knowing that we weren't alone in the darkness. We weren't the only target. But then again, in other ways, it reinforced the other fear. What if we didn't get back in time? What if we couldn't get back across the ring road? If the demonstrators were congregating at 4.30 a.m., the road would probably not be passable by 7 a.m.

As I watched the demonstrators congregate and tried to imagine the scenario in another three hours, Philip kept his eyes on the road. Every few metres sat smoking piles of burnt-out tyres. The smell was acrid. In between the tyres there were scatterings of broken glass and bricks. Philip slowed down and began weaving across the road in an effort to avoid the debris. We all felt the relief as we finally turned off the ring road and headed east once again, on the Dhulikhel road. It was our road, the road we knew. But it was different. It was pitch black. We knew what was there because we remembered it, not because we could see it.

The boys were not troubled.

'I spy with my little eye, something beginning with D,' began Chris, shading his eyes as he pressed his face up against the window pane.

'Oh, come on, Chris, you can't see anything. It's the middle of the night,' said Stephen.

'I can so,' replied Chris, undaunted. 'I can see "darkness".'

I didn't see the 'darkness'. My eyes were still seeing the 'dangers'. Up ahead I could just make out a collection of vehicles, stationary on the road. In front of the vehicles was a barbed wire barricade marking the check post out of the Kathmandu valley. On either side of the check post were soldiers manning a tank.

Philip slowed down and looked at his watch. He mumbled something to himself before pulling the van up to a stop at the end of the queue. We sat for a while and watched the scene. The soldiers were also watching. They were not letting anyone through the barricade. Philip checked his watch again before opening the van door and approaching the nearest soldier. He kept his voice low and I squinted into the darkness to keep an eye on his back. I couldn't hear their conversation. He turned while I was still watching and leapt back into the van.

'They're not letting anyone through until 5 a.m.,' he explained to me. 'From what I can make out, they're keeping the rule because the night-time curfew is still in force up here.' He paused and smiled at all of us. 'I told them that we were just a bunch of *bideshis* picking up our *saman* (belongings) but it didn't make any difference.'

I looked back out of the windows and saw the faintest glimmer of light appearing on the skyline over the terraces of paddy fields. I could just make out some of the mud houses in the distance. It was strange how in our attempts to beat the daytime curfew, we had forgotten all about the night-time curfew. It was strange how, after all this driving, it was still night.

Philip was getting restless. Every few minutes he looked down at his watch. After a while, I closed my eyes and pictured another scene. I pictured our home with the white-washed walls and the red trim, sitting halfway up our hill and surrounded by forest. In my mind, I walked through the front door and then into each room, one by one. I looked at what was in each room: the pictures and the photos on the walls, the toys and the books.

I remembered the summer's night when we had lain in our bed and watched the fireflies circle above our heads. I remembered the period in home-school when I had taught the boys to dance in their bedroom to the tune of 'I am somebody'. I remembered the mornings when we had caught Jacki and Chuck Chuck laying eggs on the cane chairs in the living room. In seeing each room, I remembered the living.

Then I wondered about Darren. Was he up yet? Had he checked all the rooms and the drawers for precious things? How would he know if it was a precious thing? I opened my eyes with a start and scanned the scene again. I needed more moments in Dhulikhel. In the distance I began to hear engines revving and a buzz of movement. It was time. The soldiers began slowly removing the barbed wire of the barricade and the vehicles made their way through. We were off again.

The biggest hurdle between the check post and Dhulikhel was the town of Banepa, the scene of some of the more violent riots in the revolution. We approached it tentatively, once again scanning for broken glass, bricks and debris. There were piles everywhere. Some of the tyres were still burning, leaving an eerie haze of smoke at eye level. Philip once again slowed down and began weaving across the road until we made it through the town safely.

Then we moved into anticipation. The dim light was picking up the distant ridges. To the right we could see the water tank on top of the house where our Irish friends had lived. To

the left we could see the turn-off to the Dhulikhel Lodge, the
site of our favourite Saturday lunches. To the right again, the
bus stop, Saru's paper shop and the lane to church. Behind
them, the red tiles that marked the roof of the Dhulikhel
Medical Institute. Back again to the left was the soccer field
and Bagmati's little vegetable shop. The vegetable shop meant
that we were nearly home.

Normally, 'nearly home' meant 'ahhh', it meant breathe out
and relax, walk slowly through the gates and smell the honeysuckle, enjoy the feel of your feet as they step over the threshold, take the load off your shoulders and find a comfortable
seat with a view . . .

Not that morning. That morning 'nearly home' meant
breathe in and get ready to race. It was 5.15 a.m. and the
starter's pistol was going off. I started gabbling to the boys
about how they should find their pillow cases and stuff them
with anything they wanted to keep. I told them that they
should say goodbye to anything that was very meaningful but
they couldn't take with them. Even as I spoke I could feel the
adrenaline as it poured through my being.

And the pistol went off. The van pulled up beside the gates
and we leapt out, ignoring the honeysuckle. We raced to the
front door and were inside before we had even breathed out.
In the hall, we almost fell over Darren who was already wheel-
ing out the four blue barrels towards the van. We shouted
greetings and the boys took the stairs three at a time, determined to be the first into their room and the first to spot the
remaining treasures. I turned right and entered the kitchen,
thinking that I would begin in the easiest room – the room
least likely to contain treasures.

I was wrong. As I moved around the concrete block that
held the gas cooker and let my eyes flicker over the bench top,
I nearly bumped into Srijana, who had come in at that moment
through the back door, emerging from the shadows of the

early morning light. I held out my hands to her and saw that her face was marked with tears. They spilled over and ran down her cheeks as she tried to speak but couldn't.

'I'm so sorry,' I repeated over and over again in Nepali.

She started to shake her head. 'I didn't want it to be like this,' she murmured, her hands trying to wipe away the tears.

'Neither did I . . .'

I was crying and hugging her and hearing the words echo around in my head. *'Make sure you say goodbye to anything that's meaningful to you and that you can't take with you'.* I couldn't take Srijana with me. In the darkness, by the gas cooker, we said goodbye.

The image of her tear-filled face slowed my otherwise manic pace up the stairs. I checked each of the bedrooms and the school room. I noticed that Darren had already packed the scrapbooks and the photos. In the boys' bedroom, all three of them were already filling their pillowcases. Jeremy's was bulging with soft toys and cars and miniature animals. I could hear the clunk of the cars as he dragged it along the floor. Chris's pillowcase seemed to be more ordered, the books flattening out the available space. On the other side of the room, Stephen was in control. He'd found his torch and his computerised Boggle. That left lots of space in the pillowcase. But, his calm noticeably evaporated when he sat down in front of his bookcase. I watched him as he stared at the rows and rows of books. I saw the look in his eyes and I understood it. How could he choose between them? How could he give up any of the stories that had been part of his world in Dhulikhel?

I didn't know. I looked around me for inspiration and found an empty box lying by the door.

'Quick!' I said. 'Throw them all in here and we'll sort them out when we get back down to Kathmandu.'

He threw them all in and we breathed again. We took one last look at the room with all the memories and then they each dragged their pillow cases out of the door and back down the stairs. The toys bounced from one to the next, sending echoes across the valley. I struggled with the box of books and followed the boys. Back outside, in the faint light of morning, Darren and Philip were already lifting the bikes in to the back of the van so that they rested on top of the barrels.

Philip was getting twitchy. 'Are you done yet?' he asked as I slid the extra box of books in beside the barrels.

'Not quite. Nearly. I'll just check the boys.'

I ran back inside the maroon gates and through the front door and wondered where they had gone. Upstairs was finished. Downstairs didn't hold the kinds of treasures that they were looking for. As I was making my way through the living area, I heard their shouts echoing around the back garden.

'Goodbye. Goodbye. Goodbye . . .' The answering calls seemed to be coming from across the valley.

I stood on the back porch and watched their moving bodies race around the garden for the last time. Jeremy was merely running in all directions, shouting. Chris had stopped and was leaning over the trunk of the orange tree and writing a goodbye letter to leave in his tree house. Stephen was checking that his fort was still well-stocked with grapefruit ammunition. He rearranged the piles for the last time and then turned away, looking vaguely satisfied. You never know when you might need a good stockpile . . .

They each arrived back on the porch, out of breath and out of sorts. I tried not to cry as we all squashed back inside the loaded van and turned around to wave at our home through the back window. It was 5.45 a.m. and the van slipped down the hill. In the same instant, our home slipped back into the time that used to be, but was no more – the time when we lived in the middle hills of the Himalayas.

The trip back down from Dhulikhel was very quiet. We didn't play I spy. We didn't try to recall. We sat and watched our town disappear. We sat and felt the life ebb out of our bodies. Outside on the road, the mood was also quiet. The check posts were open and we passed through them unhindered. It was only when we could see the ring road in the distance that we remembered the reason for our haste. The riot to end all riots. The two million people storming the palace.

As the intersection drew nearer, we leaned forward and tried to scan it for possible trouble spots. We listened for the sound of gunfire. We expected it to be jammed, impassable, frightening.

But it wasn't. There were a few groups of people standing together and talking. A dozen or so bikes wheeled silently up and down the road. It was 6.30 a.m. on Tuesday 25 April and the ring road was quiet. It was even quieter than when we had driven through it at 4.30 a.m.

'That's very strange,' we said to each other.

Fifteen minutes later, we pulled up outside the transit flat and began the task of unloading our hastily assembled possessions. As we placed them carefully in the stairwell of the transit flat, we noticed that the day's *Kathmandu Post* had just been delivered and lay open beside us on the bench. We glanced down at the headlines. They read, 'King Reinstates Parliament'.

'Wow!' said Darren, sitting down and pulling the paper towards him, hardly daring to believe it.

'That's amazing!' I responded, not entirely sure what it meant.

We read on. At midnight the night before, King Gyanendra had apparently made a royal proclamation. The *Kathmandu Post* reported the full text:

> Beloved countrymen, convinced that the source of State Authority and Sovereignty of the Kingdom of Nepal is inherent in the people of Nepal and cognisant of the spirit of the ongoing

people's movement as well as to resolve the ongoing violent conflict and other problems facing the country according to the road map of the agitating Seven Party Alliance (SPA), we, through this proclamation, reinstate the House of Representatives which was dissolved on 22 May 2002 on the advice of the then Prime Minister in accordance with the Constitution of the Kingdom of Nepal 1990. We call upon the Seven Party Alliance to bear the responsibility of taking the nation on the path to national unity and prosperity, while ensuring permanent peace and safeguarding multiparty democracy . . .

The seven parties had then responded:

Leaders of the seven-party alliance said the restoration of the House of Representatives, dissolved in May 2002, has opened the doors for resolving the current crises facing the country. After the reinstatement of the House, an all-party government will be formed to hold a dialogue with the rebels and bring them into a peaceful political process.

That's what it meant. The ten-year civil war was over. It was fantastic, unbelievable news. It was a victory to the people and an incredible answer to prayer. The people themselves were already marking it. On 25 April, what had been predicted to be a riot to end all riots quickly turned into a victory march. Later on that morning, two million people took to the streets, they gathered on the ring road but they didn't storm the palace – they didn't have to. Instead, they celebrated.

We also celebrated. At 11 a.m. we ate democracy *mo-mos* with the INF staff on the flat roof above the transit flat and we caught the mood of the celebration. We joined in the elation and listened to the relief in their speeches. Once again, the people could see a glimmer of hope for the future of their nation and they shared it with each other and with us. We poured more *chiya* into the metal cups and felt the privilege of being there in that time and that place when the tide had turned.

But at some point in the morning as the spicy *achar* (pickle) seeped into the remaining *mo-mos* on our plates, the thought did cross our minds. We didn't need to rush. We didn't need to wake up at 3.30 a.m. and race to Dhulikhel in the little green van. We didn't need to fling our treasures into pillowcases. We didn't need to abandon our home in the darkness. We didn't need to anticipate air tickets and passports. We didn't need to flee. Suddenly, with a single headline, there was nothing to flee from. Suddenly, the revolution was over.

Our energy sat suspended in the air that surrounded us. For fifteen days prior to the headline, we had been functioning in overdrive. We had been alert and twitchy to the noises and shadows around us. We had pored over news stories and embarked on wild plans to retrieve our belongings and prepared to leave the country. We had moved into the kind of constant 'help' prayers that are usually reserved for single moments of emergency. We had shared the hyper-alert state with everyone around us and, in so doing, gathered more of our own. If there was a barometer of twitchiness in Kathmandu in those days, it would have recorded unprecedented scores in the April of 2006. And it was all because we didn't know what the outcome would be. For all of April, we could only guess.

Then, suddenly, that morning, we knew the outcome. It was the outcome that we had all wanted and that we had all prayed for, but it was still, momentarily, an anticlimax. There was simply too much overdrive still pouring through our systems. There was too much hyped-up energy in the spaces that surrounded us. It was as if we had acclimatised to the uncertainties of war and we, briefly, didn't know what to do with peace. It was as if I had learnt, through practise, to see the glimmers of light within the darkness, to see the riches within the secret places – and to somehow appreciate being there. In my fears and in my lack of control and in a place that was far from my comfort zone, I had seen God's face and heard his voice. I had even learnt to see the unseen as a natural response to the seen. And it was as if I had grown so used to it that there was a part of me that almost wanted to stay there, in the darkness, where I could see the treasures.

That afternoon, I curled back up in a sunny corner of the flat and reached for my Bible. It fell open at chapter 45 of Isaiah and I re-immersed myself in the promises of God in that chapter and the following one. There were many: he will go before us and level the mountains; he will strengthen us; he will give us the treasures of the darkness; he will carry us and sustain us; he will make known the end from the beginning; he will do all that he pleases.

Indeed, in those days in Nepal it was evident that God had done all of that and more. He had heard the pleas of the Nepali Christians. Across the country they had been on their knees pleading with him to have mercy on their nation. They had fasted and prayed for his purposes in their land. They had asked for his name to be known and be on the lips of thousands. They had prayed for peace. And he had given it. Peace had come and it seemed to them to be a miracle. With tens of thousands of people on the streets demonstrating for such an extended period of time and with so many of them heavily armed, it seemed impossible that only fifteen people had died in the revolution. But these were the undisputed facts and in acknowledging them, the Christians also acknowledged the merciful hand of God. Through the facts, they pointed to him.

I turned back to the chapter before me and noticed again the double-edged nature of the promises. The promises don't sit on their own. They sit with a purpose and they always sit together. He *will* give us 'the treasures of darkness, riches stored in secret places, *so that we may know that [he is] the Lord, the God of Israel, who summons [us] by name.'* His actions always reveal his power. They always reveal his worthiness. And the more I learn to rely on him and to hear his voice in the darkness, the more I understand of his nature and the more I realise that he calls me by name.

The darkness of civil war had become, for me, a place to see treasures, to hear his voice and to acknowledge his presence and sovereignty. Beside him, there was no other. But then, when the darkness shifted suddenly with the pronouncement of peace, I was somehow aware of the shift. The questions emerged slowly. What would it be like to live in the light? Could I again learn to hear his voice and to rely on his unseen hand just as much in times of peace as in times of war?

Over the next few days, as I read the reports, I started to adjust my eyes and my energy levels. I slowly turned down overdrive and learned to sit in first gear for a bit. At the same time, Darren and I both realised that we needed to make some decisions. Having fled from our home in the darkness, we were strangely disorientated by the new state of affairs. We looked at our belongings in the stairwell and realised that we could no longer go home. There was no longer any home in Dhulikhel. Then we looked at the temporary arrangements around us. Nor was there a real home in the transit flat. We were merely there in transit, waiting for the circumstances to change and to allow us to move back to a real home somewhere else. But what if there was no real home anywhere?

We saw the emptiness in each other's eyes and reached for the calendar. Our flights to Australia were pencilled in for a date still four weeks away. After so many days of daytime curfew, four weeks seemed like an insurmountable period of time in which to exist within the vacuum. But then, Darren still had work to do. He still had lectures to give and notes to hand over. He still had purposes in being in the country. We mulled it over and then we made a compromise. We brought the flights forward by three weeks and we set concrete tasks for the remaining seven days.

One of those days was delightful. On Saturday 29 April we returned to our church in Dhulikhel and said some meaningful goodbyes – in the brightness of daylight. Our pastor finished his sermon and invited us to come up to the front. We stepped carefully through the pathway of crossed legs and found a corner close to him. He looked straight at us and his words in Nepali brought tears to my eyes.

'What we really want to say to them is, "Stay, stay, stay, please stay." We want to say it loudly and over and over again. But we can't say it. We have to be able to say goodbye and we have to be able to let them go. It's one of the hardest things that any of us can learn to do, but we have to be able to do it.'

He then motioned to everyone to stand up, and as they did they began singing together a song of farewell in Nepali. As I listened to their voices, I felt my ropes of connection with my world already twisting and fraying. Saru moved up to the front and joined me, crying. Stephen started handing out small gifts to the children. I caught a glimpse of a smile on the face of Rahel, Jalpa's daughter. I hugged her. I didn't want to let any of them go.

Our pastor was right – it's one of the hardest things to do. That morning, saying goodbye to Saru and Sanju and the children felt as if I was temporarily removing my senses. It felt as if I'd been living happily in an anchored hot air balloon for years and then suddenly someone sheared away all the ropes until my balloon began to drift impossibly out into the void, into the space called nowhere.

In the next five days, we went to four more farewell dos. We sheared off more ropes. As we made speeches, received gifts and said our goodbyes, the feelings of emptiness worsened. A decision to leave can be right and good, but that doesn't make it easy. To combat the feelings, we tried to anticipate life in Australia.

'I'm going to go to the supermarket and buy cheese.'

'I'm going to buy Weet-Bix and barbecue chicken.'

'I'm going to get my old bike out and ride to Grandma's.'

'Where's Grandma's?'

Leaving is always hard but there are moments that make it easier. The day before we were due to fly out of the country, and quite out of the blue, a Nepali physio, who had been trained in India, applied to take over Darren's job. That afternoon, in the muggy Kathmandu heat, Darren sat in on the interview and saw the full circle. He watched as Sachit signed the acceptance papers and knew that he was able to leave. The teaching notes were ready to hand over, the tutor was ready to accept them, the students were prepared, the people that we loved had been properly farewelled, and the abandoned belongings in our home had been sorted out. The time had come. We could almost hear the sounds of the engine. It was time to go.

18

A SAPPHIRE

At thirty thousand feet above the earth, the flight attendant moved the meal trolley forward and began to speak to the boys.

'On the menu today we have a choice between fish and lamb,' she said, smiling at them. 'What do you think you would like?'

Chris thought for a minute and then he turned to me. 'What's lamb, Mum?'

A moment later, Darren told Jeremy that perhaps he should begin with his salad. Jeremy looked down at his tray and inspected each item before he lifted his head.

'What's salad, Dad?'

We looked at each other. There were so many things to explain. Lamb, salad, meat pies, water from the tap, trains, escalators, traffic lights, telephone booths, dual carriageways . . . The list was so daunting that instead of addressing it we returned our gaze to the aeroplane window and saw the first glimpses of a wide, brown land below us. Within the land, tiny dirt roads made haphazard shapes in the barren landscape. The red gorges seemed unfamiliar to our eyes. They were a world away from the glistening peaks and green paddy fields that we had flown away from a mere twelve hours earlier. As we stared down at the brown earth beneath us, we felt the tension of the two worlds.

We felt the ache in the leaving and the frayed ropes in arriving. The depth of the feeling and the sounds of the emptiness almost took us by surprise. We had moved countries before and we had gone through transition before. We thought, therefore, that we would be able to do it. Perhaps we had been made complacent by the breadth of our own experience. Perhaps we had also thought that there was enough to anticipate in Australia to dispel the pain of the loss in Nepal. After all, Australia was our own country. It was full of grandparents and dear friends and comfort and playgrounds and hot water from a tap. It was the land of supermarkets and technology. It was the land of exciting new possibilities – schools for the boys and soccer teams to play for and a puppy to hug. It was even the land of safety, the place where we would be able to go out in the evening without fear of the army and where we would be able to leave for work in the morning without wondering if there was going to be a *bandh*. To us, it had remained in our minds as the land of certainty.

But now, thirty thousand feet above that heavily anticipated land, I didn't sense the certainty. I sensed the strange and the unfamiliar. I felt alienated. I was sitting above it but there were no threads drawing me down into its belly. There were no ropes connecting me or anchoring me to the land or its people. There was only a vacuum, noisy in its silence.

I reached for my journal and began to write. And as I did, I began to acknowledge God, merciful and mighty, saving and sovereign and equally so in Australia as in Nepal. If he was leading us back to Australia, then he must have purposes for us in being there and, somehow, those purposes must be as valid as our reasons for serving him in Nepal. In fact, they must be the same. I realised again that crossing geographical boundaries by aeroplane doesn't cancel out his Lordship or his sovereign acts. And so I prayed, 'Lord, in this new land, this land of outward comfort and ease, show me once again your face. Give me the treasures of the darkness in this place also, riches stored in secret places, so that I might know your truths, so that I might hear your voice, so that I might go on to follow you.'

Not long after that, the lights of Sydney came into view.

'Mum! Look down there, look at the lights!' Jeremy grabbed my arm and started pointing wildly. 'It seems just like a circus!'

It certainly did seem that way at first. As we struggled through the automatic doors with our baggage and then watched the speed of the cars on the motorway, we reached down and held on tightly to our seats. It felt as if it was all we could do to stop our heads from spinning away. As we flew along the motorway at 110 kilometres an hour, we tried to take in the rapidly changing scene. We stared at the clean gutters and the identical houses that made up the new housing developments on either side of the motorway. We felt the order and the precision of life in Sydney. We heard the silence of a street scene without the intrusion of horns and bells. After a while, the silence seeped into our bodies and relaxed us. One by one, we slipped back into the upholstery, too tired and empty to take in any more contrasts.

The plan was that we would take an extended camping holiday in order to re-familiarise ourselves slowly with the Australian way of life and at the same time recover from the stresses in Nepal. It was a good idea and it worked beautifully.

Armed with a borrowed tent and a borrowed car, we set off in a northerly direction. The skies were blue and the people were friendly. We collected shells at Byron Bay and sat watching the flocks of birds at Hervey Bay. We visited my cousin in Biloela and rode bikes in Yeppoon. We went snorkelling at the Whitsundays and marvelled at the whitest sand in the world. Along the way, we practised shopping and gradually started to read the Australian newspapers.

Mostly, we observed – but it was better than nothing. The breadth of the landscape spoke to us quietly and relaxed us. By day nineteen we felt that we could turn around and head south again.

And the car took the inland route. We stared out at the endless hectares of dusty plains, broken sporadically by clumps of eucalypts. We watched the way the horizon carried the scene – bordering and defining it, yet staying indefinably still. The red dirt that had seemed foreign to us from the aeroplane now moved closer and we felt it beneath our feet as we went in search of emus.

And that was the night that we pulled in to a town called Rubyvale, 325 kilometres west of Rockhampton. And that was when I leant over the wooden trestle and remembered the conversation that I'd had with Gillian two years earlier. As I remembered her words, her reminder that we find treasures in the darkness, I looked back down at the dirt beneath my hands and rubbed my thumb and forefinger over the tiny fragment of rock. I felt the sharpness of the edges and then, as I dropped it into the pan, I saw the gleam. It was small, but it was definitely a gleam. I moved it with the tweezers and the sunlight caught its sparkle and set it apart. A sapphire.

I called out to Darren and the boys. They came running and we passed it between us and kept turning it within our fingers, struck by the fact that we had found something so precious in a bucket of earth. Later, the office attendant peered down her microscope at our sapphire. She ummed and ahhed before she raised her head and pronounced it to be uncuttable. She said that it was too small. We watched the frown on her face and didn't mind at all. To us, it was precious because we had found it.

That night I lay in the tent after everyone else was asleep and thought about the sapphires in Rubyvale. There seemed to be two ways to find sapphires in Rubyvale: the easy way or the hard way. We could either notice them shining in a musty wall as we walked along a tunnel during a tour party or we could labour for hours with our backs to the sun and our fingers working through a pile of dirt. In both instances, though, we had made a deliberate choice to go searching. In the first case, we had seen the sparkle clearly as we glanced up during a darkened journey. But in the second case, we had deliberately laboured in the hot sun in order to find it.

The next day, as we drove further south to Carnarvon Gorge, I thought about the contrasts as well as the similarities. I thought about the intentional nature of both searches. And the more I thought about it, the more I realised that there might be a parallel in the search for the treasures of God. Perhaps, when I live in difficult times, my natural response is to look up in a dark tunnel and, in doing so, I instinctively see his truths. Feeling out of my depth, I long for his voice and in longing for it, I hear it. I hear his words to me and as I do, I embed in my life the deep and sustaining knowledge of who he is, the Lord, the God of Israel, who summons me by name. On the other hand, perhaps when I live in the sunshine of an outwardly smoother existence, I don't always feel the need to look up. The challenge then, for me, is to be more deliberate in my searching. The challenge for me is to instil in myself the discipline of the search, the often thorough and painstaking pursuit of the truths of God.

As I felt the car head south towards our new life in Australia, I was aware of my new resolution. Wherever I am, whether in war or peace, in poverty or plenty, in chaos or in comfort, I want to train myself to find the treasures. If I can't easily see them by looking upwards, I want to have the tenacity to dig them out of their crevices. I want to carve away for days and weeks until I see a tiny glimmer of a precious stone – something rich stored in a secret place. And I want to catch the sparkle as the light reflects off its facets. And then I will say in Australia as well as in Nepal, 'He is the Lord, the God of Israel, who summons me by name.' And I will give thanks.

POSTSCRIPT

The revolution of 2006 led to some significant changes in the history of Nepal. In May that year, King Gyanendra reinstated an interim government, made up of some of the ministers that had led the previous government which was dissolved in 2002. This government then took over leadership of the army, effectively taking control of the country away from the king, and the country officially became a secular state. In November 2006 a peace accord was signed between the Maoists and the interim government and the process of disarmament began. During 2007 the seven political parties and the Maoists jockeyed for power, and ethnic groups in the southern parts of Nepal protested for their rights. General elections were called twice but cancelled due to further political unrest. In April 2008, elections were held and the Maoists came into power with a landslide victory. From being the only Hindu kingdom in the world, Nepal then 'became the only country in the twenty-first century to be led by a Maoist government' (*Nepali Times*, April 2008). This ushered in a new chapter in the political history of the country and the people were once again hopeful and desperate for change. The effects of these changes remain to be seen.

GLOSSARY

Achar – pickle
Bandh – strike
Bideshi – foreigner
Bijuli – electricity
Chaddai aunnechon Yesu Raja – come quickly King Jesus
Chappals – sandals
Chiya – a sweet milky tea drink
Chowkidar – guard
Chungi – many elastic bands formed into a ball
Dal bhat – rice and lentils forming the traditional Nepali meal
Dev nagari – the script in which Nepali is written
Dinos, malai – help me
Doko – a cane basket carried on the back
Gagri – a vessel for carrying water
INF – International Nepal Fellowship
Kasto – a shawl
Khaja – Nepali snacks
Ke garne? – What should we do?
Kurta – a knee length dress worn by women with trousers underneath
Lassi – a yoghurt drink
Lungi – a wraparound skirt that reaches to the ankles
Mo-mo – spicy meat wrapped in a dumpling pastry
Moph garnos – I'm sorry

Namaste – the Nepali greeting

Oshanti – a lack of peace

Panch say rupiya – five hundred rupees

Panch rupiya – five rupees

Prabhuma sadai anand garou – always rejoice in the Lord

Puja – the process of worshipping idols

Sahuji – shopkeeper

Saman – belongings

Sari – five metres of cloth which is wrapped around the body and worn as the national dress

Shanti – peace

Shanti lagyo – feeling at peace

Teen rupiya – three rupees

Terai – the flat area of Nepal bordering India

Tika – a mark of red colouring or rice that has been placed on the forehead to indicate that *puja* has been performed

Topi – a hat

Tuk-tuk – a small three-wheeled vehicle

For more information regarding Naomi's writing and speaking ministry, please visit her website www.NaomiReed.Info and join 'My Seventh Monsoon' on Facebook.

Naomi supports the work of the International Nepal Fellowship, a Christian mission serving Nepali people through health and development work. For more information go to www.inf.org

**INTERNATIONAL
NEPAL
FELLOWSHIP**

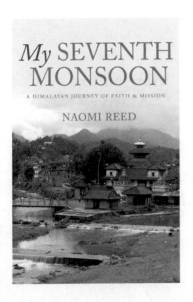

My Seventh Monsoon

A Himalayan Journey of Faith and Mission

Naomi Reed

'The seventh monsoon was the hardest of them all. I sat on the back porch of our Himalayan home and stared as the rain streamed down all around me. I had never felt so hemmed in – by the constant rain, by the effects of the civil war and by the demands of home-school. As I sat there and listened to the pounding on our tin roof, I wondered whether I would make it through. I wondered whether I would cope with another 120 days of rain. And in doing so, I began to long for another season . . .'

From the view point of her seventh monsoon, Naomi Reed takes time to look back on the seasons of her life. As she does so, she shares with us her journey of faith and mission and reveals poignant truths about God and the way he works his purposes in our lives through seasons.

978-1-86024-828-3

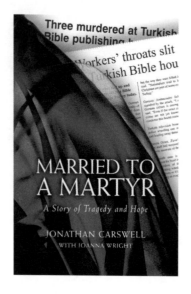

Married to a Martyr

A Story of Tragedy and Hope

Jonathan Carswell
with Joanna Wright

It was Wednesday afternoon and already rumours of a terrible, triple murder were circulating around the world. Without a doubt, something horrific had happened but reports were sketchy at best, frequently embellished and exaggerated.

As hearsay was replaced with hard evidence it was clear that Susanne Geske had become a martyr's widow, far from home, in Malatya, eastern Turkey.

With so many aggrandised stories being told as fact, this book seeks the truth from the one person who could provide it with complete authority. This is the remarkable story of Susanne Geske . . .

978-1-85078-785-3

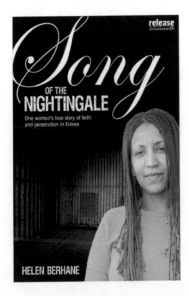

Song of the Nightingale

One Woman's Dramatic Story of Faith and Persecution in Eritrea

*Helen Berhane
with Emma Newrick*

The true story of Helen Berhane, held captive for more than two years in appalling conditions in her native Eritrea. Her crime? Sharing her faith in Jesus and refusing – even though horrendously tortured – to deny him. A sobering, painful and heart-rending account of true faith in the face of evil, this book makes for uncomfortable and yet inspirational reading.

Helen says, 'I want to give a message to those of you who are Christians and live in the free world: you must not take your freedom for granted . . . If I could sing in prison, imagine what you can do for God's glory with your freedom.' A real challenge for the church in the West.

978-1-85078-864-5

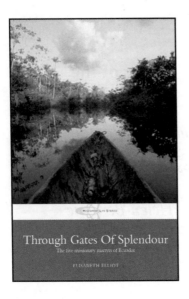

Through Gates of Splendour

The Five Missionary Martyrs of Ecuador

Elisabeth Elliot

In 1956 the world was stunned by a shocking event . . .

'Mary was standing with her head against the radio, her eyes closed. After a while she spoke "They found one body . . ."'

Missionary history will never let us forget the five young American men savagely martyred by Auca Indians in the jungles of Ecuador as they attempted to reach them with the word of God.

Elisabeth Elliot, widow of one of these men, records the story of their courage and devotion to Christ in the face of danger and difficulty.

978-1-85078-034-2